the big book of
greetings
cards

the big book of
greetings
cards

over 40 step-by-step projects

vivienne bolton

NEW
HOLLAND

Dedication

For 14-year old Chloe.
Kind, tolerant, understanding, thoughtful, wise, funny, original Chloe.

Published in 2002 by
New Holland Publishers (UK) Ltd
London · Cape Town · Sydney · Auckland

Garfield House
86–88 Edgware Road
London
W2 2EA
United Kingdom
www.newhollandpublishers.com

80 McKenzie Street
Cape Town 8001
South Africa

Level 1, Unit 4, 14 Aquatic Drive
Frenchs Forest, NSW 2086
Australia

218 Lake Road
Northcote, Auckland
New Zealand

ISBN 1 85974 993 3

Senior Editor: Clare Hubbard
Editor: Gillian Haslam
Production: Hazel Kirkman
Design: Peter Crump
Photographer: Shona Wood
Editorial Direction: Rosemary Wilkinson

3 5 7 9 10 8 6 4

Reproduction by Modern Age Repro House Ltd, Hong Kong
Printed and bound by Times Offset (M) Sdn. Bhd., Malaysia

Note

The author and publishers have made every effort to ensure that all
instructions given in this book are safe and accurate, but they cannot accept
liability for any resulting injury or loss or damage to either property or
person, whether direct or consequential and howsoever arising.

Acknowledgements

Designing and making such a wide variety of cards for this book has been quite a
challenge. I would like to thank my editor, Clare Hubbard who has been calm,
organized and kept her sense of humour throughout. Thanks also to Shona Wood
whose photography complemented my work so well and to Rosemary Wilkinson
at New Holland, who had the idea for this book in the first place.

contents

introduction

I have enjoyed card-making as a hobby for many years and consider a handmade greetings card a gift in itself. Every Christmas I take on the challenge of creating just the right card that can be produced in large numbers to send to faraway friends, and each new year brings new celebrations, such as birthdays, weddings and births, and with them come new opportunities for my creative skills. I have also spent many pleasant evenings making cards to put away for later use. Nowadays handmade cards have become quite fashionable and can be found on the shelves of most gift shops, but they can cost a pretty penny. I hope that the ideas in this book will inspire you to make your own greetings cards.

There are so many crafts and skills which can be used to decorate greetings cards. Some are simple and suited to mass production, for example stencilled Christmas cards, while others are more time-consuming and intricate and best for a one-off card to celebrate a special event. With card-making as a hobby, you have the perfect excuse to collect and use beautiful handmade and printed papers, sparkling sequins and ribbons and coloured glitter and glitz. By keeping an on-going collection of inspirational bits and pieces, you will always have at hand what you need to create cards for every occasion.

While Christmas is my busiest card production period, birthday and thank-you cards are what I enjoy making most.

Thinking up just the right idea for a friend's fortieth birthday can be quite a challenge and thank-you cards bring the opportunity for creating memory style cards. I once made a lovely thank-you card for a friend using the theatre programme, ticket stubs and chocolate wrappers as memories of a lovely evening out. Making romantic cards can be very rewarding, and wedding and engagement greetings are always an inspiration – although I'm still waiting to receive that special Valentine handmade by a man! You can also use the ideas shown here for making gift tags and invitations.

I have tried to include as many crafts as possible in this book – collage, stamping, punching, stencilling, quilling and cross stitch, to mention but a few. Try out the ideas and then use them as a springboard for your own creativity. Be inspired and adventurous, create your own masterpieces, become a collector of fine papers and 'useful things' and, most important of all, enjoy a hobby your friends and relatives will share.

Vivienne Bolton

getting started

Once you get hooked on card-making, it's a good idea to invest in a large folder in which to store special papers, plus a box file for holding smaller sheets. I have a 'useful box' of paints, brushes, glues, erasers, measuring tools and all the paraphernalia one collects as time goes by. Paper and card, pencils and paints, glitter, glue and a jumble of decorative bits and pieces – anything from a pretty feather collected on holiday to a photograph of a new baby, from pressed flowers and leaves collected from the garden to ribbon once tied around a present – can all be found in my box.

When getting started with any new hobby, equipping yourself with the basic tools and materials is part of the fun. Making a greetings card can be as quick and simple or as time-consuming and intricate as you want it to be. Over a period of time and as you work your way through the various ideas in this book, you will find you collect an interesting range of equipment and stock of paper and card. So, when the occasion arises, you have everything you need to hand to create a perfect greetings card.

This first chapter demonstrates all the basic techniques required, including transferring designs, scoring, folding and cutting and provides information on the different types of paper, card and other basic materials. Special techniques and equipment for individual cards are detailed in the projects that follow.

paper and card

There is an such an abundance of printed and plain, handmade and commercially produced paper available now that it can be difficult to know where to start. Most commercially produced paper and card comes in standard sizes, graded from A1 to A5 (A4 is the standard size for most letterhead paper).

Most of the projects in this book are made using A4 (210 x 297mm / 8¼ x 11¹¹⁄₁₆in) and A5 (148 x 210mm / 5¹³⁄₁₆ x 8¼in) size sheets purchased from art and craft material suppliers.

Good stationery and art and craft suppliers generally carry a wide range of plain paper. This is usually ready cut to A4 size and available for purchase by the sheet. Paper and card is available in a seemingly limitless range of colours, weights, qualities and textures, from the lightweight, finest tissue to heavy embossed handmade paper.

I impulse-buy sheets of handmade and printed paper and save pretty gift-wrap or packaging which I think may be suitable for a greetings card. Coloured paper can be purchased by the sheet or in pads. Keep a look out for small pads of paper in rainbow colour selections.

Consider the thickness of paper or card when choosing sheets for particular projects. Thin card or folded cartridge paper is more suitable for a card base (known as a 'blank') with further decorative layers cut from lighter paper. If you choose gift-wrap for a card blank, make sure you fold a double layer or glue it to plain card to give the card some substance.

Sugar paper

This paper is thick, has a slight texture to it, comes in lovely muted colours and is economically priced. Because it is such good value for money, it is a good card to use to practise your techniques on. The thickness means you will need a double layer if using sugar paper to create a card base, but nevertheless it is a very useful paper to have in stock.

Corrugated card and paper

Commercially corrugated card is the most adventurous medium. It can bring texture and depth to greetings cards and is certainly worth purchasing. It can be used to make the card blank or to create decorative elements.

Handmade paper

Using handmade paper brings a natural look to your cards. The prettiest papers have flower petals embedded in them. It can be used to create the card blank, as a panel on a plain card base or to create decorative elements. Mulberry paper is a light, opaque paper that is handmade from mulberry leaves and contains strands of silk. It comes in a wide variety of colours and shades and is useful for building up layered cards.

Tissue paper

Once only available in blue and white, tissue paper now comes in rainbow colours and you can often find printed tissue paper as well. Tissue paper is good to stencil or print on but is not suitable to be used as a card blank, unless backed with a more substantial paper.

Translucent paper

This is a fairly modern invention and is lovely to use when creating layered effects as you can see through it. It softens the lines of any patterns on underlying layers.

Metallic paper

Metallic paper and foil are good highlighters and can be used to create great borders. Some metallic papers and foils are thicker and shinier than others. White paper with flecks of silver and gold can create a stylish finish to a card.

Taking care of your paper

Take good care of your stock of paper and card. Be sure to store card and paper flat to prevent possible damage. If paper does become creased it can often be ironed flat with a warm iron and restored to near-perfect condition. If the whole sheet cannot be saved, keep the good bits for small projects, collages or layering.

Organize your paper by size – I find most greetings cards I make start off with an A5 card base, so I like to keep my A5 card and paper stacked together. If you collect a large quantity of paper you might like to file it by colour.

pens, pencils and paints

Felt tip pens

Felt tip pens come in a variety of thicknesses and a rainbow of colours. I have a set of fine point felt tip pens, a set of broad tipped pens and a set of paint pens. Felt tip pens make good border markers, can be used for highlighting and for writing special messages in cards. They can also be used to colour rubber stamps in different colours in place of a single colour ink pad.

Marker pens

I use these when creating 'painted glass' images and in a variety of other ways. A double-ended fine point/broad point pen is useful to have.

Gel pens

These are a wonderful invention and I use them a lot. The quality of the ink is very good and the colours are amazing. I enjoy using gel pens on dark paper and card.

Silver and gold marker pens

Metallic colours can be used to great effect on both light and dark backgrounds. I have a couple of fine line pens as well as some broad tipped ones. It is important to replace the lid immediately after use.

Pencils

I prefer to use an HB for general use and a softer 3B for drawing lines which I will later

erase when trying out designs. A good, clean eraser is also important.

Paint

A simple watercolour paint box is useful to have. I also have a selection of acrylic paints. Gold and silver acrylic colours come in a variety of shades – choose the more glittery golds for special effect. Use good quality paint brushes that do not leave hairs on the paper after painting.

equipment

Scissors

You will need different types of scissors for cutting different surfaces, so invest in large and small paper scissors, tiny embroidery scissors for cutting out intricate shapes, scissors reserved for cutting fabric and scissors with a patterned edge, such as wavy-edged scissors. Keep scissors and knives in a safe spot and out of the reach of children.

Craft knife

A good, sharp craft knife is essential for cutting neat edges. Keep a supply of new blades readily available. They are very sharp and great care should be taken when using them. Always use a metal ruler when cutting straight edges with knives and always work on a cutting board. Craft knives need to be sharp and consequently can be dangerous weapons in the wrong hands. Always sheath knives not in use. Wherever possible, cut away from your body.

Rulers and measuring

It is worth investing in a metal ruler for cutting against and a small clear plastic ruler for taking measurements. A set square is essential for measuring accurate right angles and this is vital when making greetings cards.

adhesives

You will need a range of different glues when card-making, including:

PVA glue

PVA glue or white glue which becomes transparent when dry is useful for sticking paper to card or card to card. It is often easiest to pour a small blob of glue onto a piece of scrap card and apply it with either a cotton bud or cocktail stick.

Glue stick

A glue stick is essential and is useful for sticking paper to paper or for sticking glitter or embossing powder to card or paper. You should also be able to obtain fine tipped glue sticks which are useful for attaching sequins and beads. Keep your glue stick clean and remember to replace the lid after use.

Spray adhesive

Spray adhesive is useful for attaching fabric and tissue paper. You will also need a 'glue box' – this is a cardboard carton approximately 40cm (16in) square. Position the item to be spray-glued in the bottom of the box, spray the adhesive then close the lid of the box to minimize inhalation of fumes. Remove after a few minutes and the item is ready for sticking down. Always follow manufacturer's instructions.

Glitter glue

This can be used to attach acetate decoratively.

Sticky tape

Sticky tape comes in a selection of widths. I prefer to use a clear, low-tack tape for best results. Double-sided tape can be used instead of glue.

other bits and pieces

Stamps

Stamps come in such a wide variety of styles that the selection seems endless. The craft of stamping has a multitude of applications to card-making. Use coloured pens and sparkling embossing powders to create unique effects for special cards and simple coloured ink pads and interesting stamps to mass produce Christmas cards or party invitations.

Punches

These come in a variety of patterns and shapes and are used to punch decorative patterns and motifs into paper. The pattern or shape that has been punched from the paper can be used to decorate cards, gift tags and envelopes.

Glitter

Glitter or sparkle is available in small quantities in bags or plastic cylinders and comes in a variety of qualities and colours. I find the finer glitter best for card decoration. I sometimes use embossing powder as glitter as it is so fine and sparkly. A glue stick provides a good bed for glitter or embossing powder.

Precision heat tool

A heat tool is necessary to activate and fix embossing powder. These tools get extremely hot so you must be careful when using them, keeping your hands and the paper or card that is being heated a safe distance away from the heat source. Always read and carefully follow the manufacturer's instructions.

Sewing equipment

A selection of needles and threads are useful when completing projects involving fabrics and ribbons.

card-making techniques

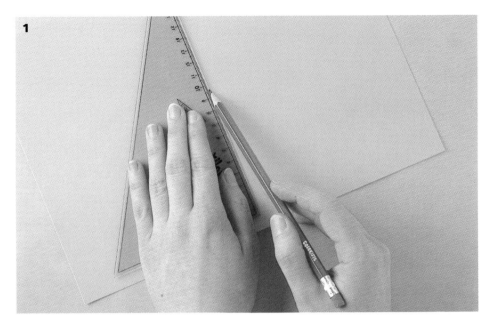

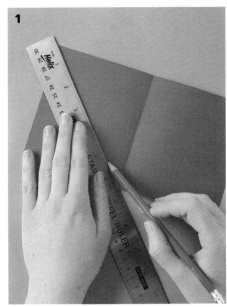

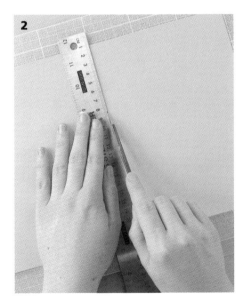

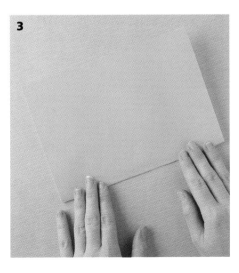

Cutting and scoring

Scoring makes folding card and paper easy and gives your finished cards a professional appearance. You will need a craft knife, metal ruler and cutting board to score or cut card or heavy paper. Take great care when using craft knives as they are very sharp and always cut against a metal ruler.

1 Find the central fold line using a ruler and set square. Mark lightly with a pencil.

2 Gently draw the craft knife along the line on the outside of the card, only just cutting through the surface to score the card.

3 Fold the card inwards and press firmly along the fold.

Cutting a window

It does take practice to cut a window neatly, particularly a round or oval window. Ready-cut card blanks are available from art and craft suppliers. Windows cut into cards have a variety of decorative uses. They can frame a special photograph or piece of needlework or simply add interest to an otherwise simple design.

1 Open out a scored and folded card blank. To find the centre of the front of the card,

use a light touch to draw a diagonal line from the upper right corner to the lower left corner; then from the upper left corner to the lower right corner. The midpoint of the card will be the point at which the lines cross.

2 Once you have decided on the size and shape of the window, mark up with a pencil and ruler. For example, if you wanted a central square window 8 x 8cm (3¼ x 3¼ in) you would measure 4cm (1½in) to the right and left, and above and below the midpoint. Rule lines to create the square to be cut out.

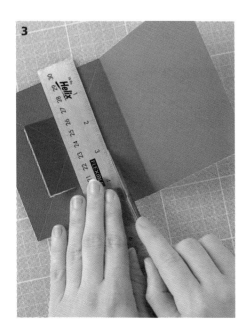

3 Use a craft knife and metal ruler to cut out the window.

4 For circular windows, draw the circle using a pair of compasses. You may find it easier to use scissors rather than a craft knife to cut out circles. Begin by using a craft knife to slash a cross in the centre of the circle, then cut out with scissors.

Tearing paper

Tearing paper can produce an interesting and decorative edging for a project. Measure and mark up the line to be torn. Fold and then tear against a ruler.

It is best to wet handmade paper before tearing. To do this, measure and mark up the line, then, use a fine brush to 'paint' water along the line to be torn. When the water has soaked into the paper, tear carefully. If you do not want the edge of the paper to be too rough, tear along the edge of a ruler. The paper can be ironed dry using a warm iron to steam away the water and smooth the paper.

Transferring patterns

At the back of this book you will find templates to be used in a number of the projects (see pages 134 to 141). These can be transferred in a number of ways.

Photocopy the template you wish to use and cut out before using as a pattern. This can be useful if you wish to make the pattern larger or smaller as the photocopier can do this for you. Alternatively, trace over the image either using tracing paper (available in art and craft shops) or kitchen baking paper. The third option is to use a special carbon tracing paper which can be purchased from craft shops.

making envelopes

Although most of the projects are a suitable size for commercially available envelopes, it is often more appropriate to create a matching envelope for a handmade card. Making an envelope is a fairly easy task and the advantage of a homemade envelope is that it will co-ordinate with your card.

How to make an envelope

You will need
Sheet of paper approximately three times the width of your card
Scissors
Pencil
Metal ruler
Glue stick

1 Place the greetings card centrally on the bottom edge of the sheet of paper. Fold the sheet of paper down over the greetings card. Open up the sheet of paper.

2 Place the card along the fold line you have just created. Fold the paper up over the greetings card (it should cover the card). Next, fold the paper down over the greetings card.

3 Open up both folds. Now fold the side sections of paper inwards over the card. Open up the two new folds. You should now have four fold lines.

4 Place the sheet of paper onto a cutting board, and using a craft knife and metal ruler, cut away the four rectangular

sections marked by the fold lines in each corner of the sheet of paper. You should be left with two large flaps on either side of the central section. These flaps will become your tabs.

5 Use the pencil to mark up 1cm (½in) wide tabs on each flap. Use the craft knife to trim away the excess paper.

6 Fold the lower section of the card upwards and use a glue stick to stick the tabs down over what will form the back of the envelope. When you have placed the greetings card in the envelope, fold the upper back of the envelope down over the card and use a glue stick to seal your envelope. If liked, you can shape the upper flap as shown on page 16.

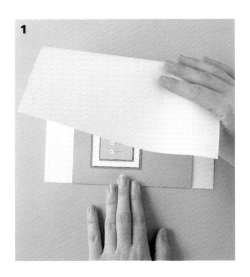

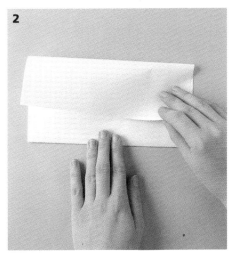

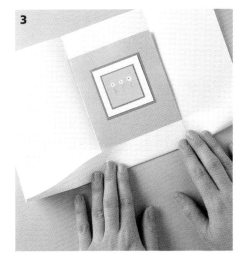

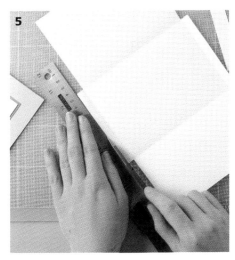

Padded envelopes

A piece of bubble wrap or wadding covered with tissue paper attached inside the envelope can be used to protect textured or gift cards.

Lined envelopes

Lining an envelope is easy to do. When you have cut out your envelope shape use it as a template and cut a lining 5mm (¼in) smaller all around than the envelope. Use spray adhesive to attach to the inside before gluing the envelope into shape. Tissue paper works well as a lining.

Decorating envelopes

Practise with different types of envelope flaps on plain paper. You will find envelope making can be highly creative. Depending on the design of the card you might want to use the same paper or a co-ordinating shade. The envelope could be decorated with a similar design or left plain. Embossing powder, cut outs or stencils are all effective forms of decoration.

Almost all the techniques found in this book can be used to decorate envelopes. If you make envelopes from gift-wrap, it may be a good idea to stick a plain white label on the front on which to write the address so that it is clear.

pressing flowers and leaves

I often use pressed flowers and leaves to decorate cards. Choose light foliage and flowers for pressing as anything too 'fleshy' may go mouldy during the drying process. Commercially available presses are good but I find using an old book more romantic and it works just as well.

Place the flowers and leaves between layers of white cartridge paper and place inside the book. Close the book and weigh it down with some more heavy tomes, then leave for a couple of weeks for a good result. The delicate shades of pressed flowers can make quite beautiful cards, while autumn leaves seem to retain their colours making them highly decorative. A pressed rose from a wedding bouquet would look wonderful on a first anniversary card and often the smaller garden flowers, leaves and seed heads make good decoration when pressed and dried.

displaying your cards

Greetings cards make a lovely display. For many years my Christmas cards hung on lines of gold ribbon strung around the room. Cards also look good attached to streamers of ribbon decorated with bows or randomly placed on a noticeboard. Don't limit displays of cards to the living room – they look just as good strung up in the kitchen or along the sideboard in the dining room.

Easter cards can be hung on a branch of spring blossom or amongst the pots of spring flowering bulbs on a sunny window sill. Birthday greetings should stay on display for at least a week, extending celebrations for everyone.

When the celebrations are finally over why don't you make a Christmas collage of the cards you have received or a special memory board for birthday cards? I have a display of special birthday cards received over the years, cards my children made at school and a special Valentine, along with cards made by friends. I have put them in simple clip frames and they decorate a quiet corner of the living room as a reminder of just what good friends and talented children I have.

paperwork

projects

celebration collage

This card is effortlessly simple to make and requires only the most basic materials. Artfully placed scraps of torn sugar paper and snippets of gold foil make up this colourful celebration collage.

you will need

- A5 sheet of blue handmade paper
- Pale green, red, yellow, dark green and purple sugar paper
- Metal ruler
- Glue stick
- Scissors
- Scraps of gold and green foil or recycled chocolate wrappers
- Black outliner

timing Once you have gathered a selection of papers together, this card does not take long to make.

message Suitable for almost every occasion.

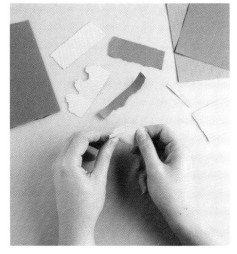

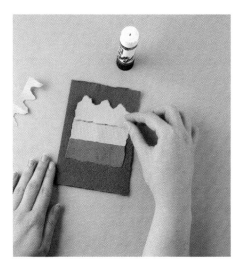

1 Fold the sheet of blue handmade paper in half to create the basic card shape. Tear an 8 x 3cm (3¼ x 1¼in) piece from the pale green and the red sugar paper. Next, tear a piece of yellow sugar paper 8 x 3cm (3¼ x 1¼in). Fold it in three and tear off the corners from one end.

2 Open out the folded yellow paper. Using the photo as a guide, glue all three pieces of torn sugar paper in place on the card.

3 Tear three narrow strips of dark green sugar paper and glue in place on top of the pale green rectangle. Next tear a simple 8 x 3cm (3¼ x 1¼in) rectangle from the purple sugar paper and then carefully tear out the wriggly shape. Glue in place on top of the yellow paper. Use scissors to cut out a simple 8 x 2cm (3¼ x ¾in) pattern from gold foil and glue at the base of the collage.

4 Cut three small triangular shapes from gold foil and glue at the top of the yellow panel. Cut out a narrow strip of gold foil and glue at the bottom of the green panel. Tear three 1cm (½in) squares of red paper and glue diagonally on the green panel. Place a small square of green foil on the centre of each square. Stick tiny snippets of gold foil around the edge of the card. Make five crosses from the gold foil and glue them on to the red paper. Highlight the collage with black outliner.

Use miniature collages as gift tags.

a touch of spice

Layers of orange and brown mulberry paper mounted on speckled card and richly edged in gold

create a perfect setting for star anise, a spice from the mysterious East. This stylishly simple card

will delight the senses with texture, colour and fragrance.

you will need

- A5 sheet of speckled card
- Mulberry paper in brown and orange
- Pencil and metal ruler
- Scissors
- Glue stick
- Sheet of lightweight white paper
- Gold outliner
- Clear adhesive
- Star anise pod

timing This card will not take long to make; you may find yourself making a few more cards to save for later.

message Send this card to a well-travelled friend and see if they recognize the spice.

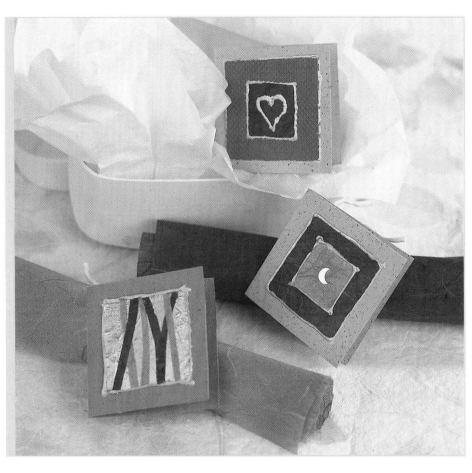

Tags made using similar colours but different designs are very effective.

1 Fold the speckled card in half to make the card blank. Measure out a piece of brown mulberry paper 8.5 x 7cm (3¼ x 2¾in) and cut out. Use the glue stick to attach the paper to the card in a high central position.

2 Glue a piece of orange mulberry paper to a sheet of lightweight white paper. From this cut a 5 x 5cm (2½ x 2½in) square. Use the glue stick to attach it in a high central position on top of the brown paper.

3 Create borders around the brown and orange paper with the gold outliner. Use the clear adhesive to attach the star anise. If you wish, make an envelope from mulberry paper layered over a more substantial paper.

newborn baby

Four baby's nappies pegged up on a silver washing line flutter across the sky, surrounded by tiny teddy bears, all set in richly textured card. This magical newborn baby card will delight a mother or grandmother at this special time.

Make these dainty gift tags from scraps of handmade paper and silver bits and pieces.

you will need

- Textured white card
- Pencil and metal ruler
- Craft knife
- Cutting board
- Lilac handmade paper
- Glue stick
- Scissors

- Scrap of silver thread
- PVA glue
- White tissue paper
- Slivers of wood (a matchstick would do)
- Silver teddy bear confetti shapes
- Tweezers

timing This imaginative card will take no time at all to make.

message Send this card to a new mother with a message of love.

1 Cut a card blank 24 x 12cm (9½ x 4¾in) from the sheet of white textured card. Fold in half. Next, cut a piece of handmade paper 10 x 10cm (4 x 4in). Use a glue stick to attach it centrally to the front of the card.

2 Cut a length of silver thread. Put a spot of PVA glue onto a piece of scrap card and lightly pull the thread through the glue. Carefully lay the thread across the card, so it loops across the sky. Trim the ends level with the lilac square.

3 Glue together a double layer of white tissue paper. Cut some small nappy shapes from the double layer and 'hang' them on the line using a glue stick.

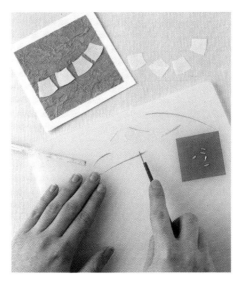

4 Use the craft knife to slice some tiny slivers of matchstick wood and glue them to the nappies to represent the clothes pegs.

5 Use PVA glue to attach six silver teddy bears to the front of the card. It is easiest to do this by holding the bears with the tweezers, touching them into the glue and then placing them on the card.

good luck wish

This card has a sense of the Orient, with the black card providing a mysterious background for the opulent reds and golds. This good luck symbol was cut using a commercial punch. Have a look around your local craft and art shops for something similar, or try one of the mail-order suppliers. I have also made and decorated a co-ordinating envelope and gift tags.

you will need

- A5 sheet of black card
- Pencil and metal ruler
- Handmade speckled red paper
- Scissors
- Glue stick
- A5 sheet of lightweight white paper
- Paper punch with good luck symbol
- A5 sheet of black paper
- A5 sheet of gold mottled card
- A5 sheet of red paper

timing Once you have located a suitable punch, this card is simple and quick to make.

message Send a good luck greeting to a friend about to sit an exam. This card also makes a very stylish birthday greeting.

1 Fold the black card in half to create the card blank. Cut out a 5 x 5cm (2 x 2in) square from the red handmade paper and use the glue stick to attach it to the lightweight white paper. Cut carefully around the edges.

2 Insert the glued-together red and white paper into the punch and cut out the shape.

3 Cut out a square around the shape and glue a small piece of black paper to the reverse side of the symbol. Next, glue this onto a piece of gold card measuring 6 x 6cm (2½ x 2½in).

4 Cut a 7 x 7cm (2¾ x 2¾in) square from the red paper and glue this behind the gold card. Using the glue stick, attach the prepared motif in a high central position on the greetings card.

5 Make a matching envelope (see page 15). Punch a good luck symbol on the back flap and back the cut-out with black paper. Punch another symbol in one of the bottom corners of the envelope.

6 Slide the card into the envelope so that the black of the card shows through the punched holes.

pretty in pink

Send this card as a birthday greeting, a romantic note or simply to say hello to a friend. Using

pretty pink translucent paper over rose pink card and decorated with silver gel pen, it is incredibly

simple and quick to make. You might want to draw different shaped balloons more appropriate

to the greeting, for example circles or stars.

you will need

- A5 sheet of pink card
- Pencil and metal ruler
- Set square
- Craft knife
- Cutting board
- Scissors
- Pink translucent paper
- Glue stick
- Silver gel pen

 timing This is so quick and easy to make that you might like to try a few ideas of your own using translucent paper and metallic pens.

message This stylish card can be used to send almost any greeting.

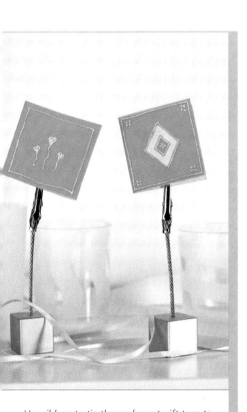

Use ribbon to tie these elegant gift tags to pink tissue paper-wrapped presents.

1 Measure a rectangle 21 x 10cm (8½ x 4in) on the pink card. Cut out and fold in half. This is your basic card. Cut a piece of pink translucent paper to the same size. Fold in half, then open up.

2 Use the ruler to measure out a window 5.5 x 5.5cm (2¼ x 2¼in) in the centre of the front of the translucent paper (see page 13).

3 Use a craft knife to carefully cut out the window in the translucent paper. Keep the square you have cut out.

4 Run the glue stick down the spine of the pink card and fix it inside the folded translucent paper.

5 Use a silver gel pen to draw swirl shapes and a freehand silver border around the cut-out square.

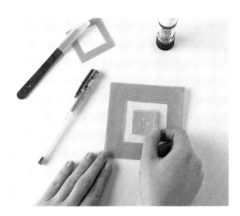

6 Using the 'window' of translucent paper you removed earlier, cut out a square shape roughly 3 x 3cm (1¼ x 1¼in). Attach centrally using the glue stick. Use the silver gel pen to draw on three heart-shaped balloons and a border.

Christmas window

Photocopying onto acetate can create really beautiful images, perfect for card-making. Take photographs of leaves against a background of sky or lay them on a sheet of plain white card. Images with a light background and a strong central image work best. Here I have chosen holly leaves for a sophisticated, seasonal card.

you will need

- Acetate photo-copies of image
- Pencil and metal ruler
- Set square
- Craft knife
- Cutting board
- A5 sheet of white card
- Silver glitter glue
- Scissors
- Double-sided tape
- A5 sheet of white paper
- Glue stick

timing Once you have the acetate copies made, this card takes no time at all to assemble.

message A good card to mass-produce to send Christmas greetings to friends and family.

1 The image area needs to be 7.5 x 7.5cm (3 x 3in). Choose the best photocopied image and trim it to size.

2 Cut a piece of white card 10 x 21cm (4 x 8½in). Score and fold in half. This is the card blank.

3 To create the central window, mark a 2cm (¾in) border all around the front of the card and carefully cut out the central square using a craft knife.

4 Spread a little silver glitter glue around the border on the front of the card. Leave to dry.

The holly and the ivy; seasonal gift tags.

5 Attach the acetate to the back of the window using double-sided adhesive tape.

6 Cut a piece of white paper into a rectangle 9.5 x 20cm (3¾ x 8in) and fold in half. Apply a small line of glue down the inside spine of the card and stick the inner leaf in position.

host of angels

These stylish cut-and-fold paper angels will look great on the mantelpiece at Christmas. Paper-cutting is always a favourite with children, so get them involved and see what they come up with. Once you have made the template this card is quick and easy to make, so start a production line and make them for all your friends.

you will need

- Pencil
- Tracing paper
- Scissors
- A4 sheet of white cartridge paper
- Gold marker pen
- A4 sheet of gold paper
- Glue stick

 timing Quick and easy to make.

message Paper cut-outs are great fun to make – you may want to make all your Christmas cards this way next season.

1 Use a pencil and tracing paper to trace the angel template on page 134. Cut around the tracing to make the template. Fold a sheet of white A4 cartridge paper in half, then open flat. Now fold from each side in towards the centre and run your finger along the folds to flatten them. Re-fold the centre to create a zigzag fold with four sections.

2 Place the angel template on the front of the folded sheet. Use the pencil to draw around the shape.

3 Cut out the angel, making sure you do not trim the folds where the hands and the bottom of the skirts meet – these points hold the card together. Open out.

4 To decorate the angels, use the gold pen to draw an outline and to add the details (see the photo on page 32 for guidance).

5 Fold the gold paper into a four-section zigzag (as in step 1). The width of the folds should be the same as the width of the angels, but the depth of the card needs to be approximately 2cm (¾in) greater. Trim if necessary.

6 Use the glue stick to attach the angel cut-outs to the gold paper, carefully matching the fold lines. Re-fold the card to fit into an envelope.

decorate the tree

Corrugated card comes in a variety of colours and the size of the corrugations can vary. Two styles of corrugated card are used to make this bright seasonal card. To emphasize the textures, I have used a very simple Christmas tree design decorated with foil stars. I cut the red card so that the lines run horizontally, but you could change the direction of the lines if you wish.

you will need

- Red corrugated card
- Pencil and ruler
- Craft knife
- Cutting board
- Tracing paper
- Green handmade paper
- Brown corrugated card
- Glue stick
- Tweezers
- Gold and red foil stars
- Glue pen

 timing Quick to make, but gluing on the stars will slow you down a little.

message A very stylish Christmas card.

1 Measure a 14 x 14cm (5½ x 5½in) square of red corrugated card. Cut the square out using a craft knife. Trace the template on page 134. Lay the template directly on the card with the top of the tree 3cm (1¼in) from the top of the card and, using a craft knife, cut the triangle as far as the fold line. Fold the card into shape.

2 Cut out the original tracing. Use the templates to cut out the tree from green paper and the pot from brown corrugated card. It is best to draw on the reverse side of the paper and card.

3 Using the glue stick, neatly glue the tree and pot in position on the front of the card.

4 Using tweezers, pick up the foil stars, run them over the tip of the glue pen and stick them in position on the Christmas tree.

Make gift tags using different types of corrugated card.

gardener's memory album

Decoupage and flower-pressing are great hobbies, and come together to make an excellent card for a gardening friend. This is the ideal card to send to someone with green fingers, and you might like to enclose a real packet of seeds!

you will need

- A5 sheet of aubergine-coloured card
- Pencil and metal ruler
- Craft knife
- Cutting board
- A4 sheet of thin brown card
- Set square
- Glue stick
- Suitably decorated gift-wrap
- Selection of dried flowers
- Tracing paper
- Thin brown paper
- Seeds

timing Collecting the various elements of this card together is what takes the time.

message Send greetings to your gardening friends. You can make this card as seasonal as you like by varying the gift-wrap.

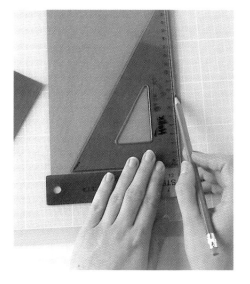

1 Score and fold the aubergine-coloured card in half to create the card base. From the thin brown card, measure and cut a piece 20 x 14cm (8 x 5½in), score and fold in half. Using a glue stick, glue on top of the aubergine-coloured card, matching up the fold lines.

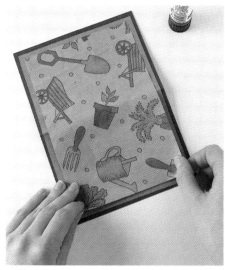

2 Measure and cut a piece of gift-wrap 19 x 13cm (7½ x 5in). Consider which elements of the gift-wrap design you would like to see on the card before you do this. Be sure to save a motif to decorate the centre of the card. Glue this centrally on top of the thin brown card.

3 Next, measure a piece of thin brown card 8.5 x 10.5cm (3¼ x 4¼in) and use the craft knife and cutting board to cut it out. Spread the back with glue and attach centrally on the front of the card. Cut a suitable motif from the gift-wrap and use the glue stick to attach it on the lower left hand side of the card. Add a spray of dried flowers to the right-hand edge of the card.

4 Now make the seed packet. Trace the template on page 134. Cut the seed packet shape from brown paper, fold into shape and use the glue stick to hold in place. Glue the seed packet onto the top left-hand side of the card. Use a small quantity of glue to attach a few seeds, as if they have spilled out of the open packet.

looking through the garden gate

This pretty card is made using shaped pieces of coloured paper to create a simple

yet very effective image. Once you have made this card, why not try to create your

own design?

you will need

- Tracing paper
- Pencil
- Spray adhesive
- Scrap of card for template
- Scissors

- A5 sheet of textured white card
- Paper in yellow, purple, dove grey, lilac, green and violet
- Glue stick

 timing Paper-cutting takes time and patience, so make this card when you have plenty of time and won't feel rushed.

message Send birthday greetings on this handsome card.

1 Trace the template of the lady on page 135 onto tracing paper. Using spray adhesive, attach the tracing paper to a piece of scrap card and cut around the shape of the lady.

2 Fold the white card in half to form the card blank. Trace around the whole template on yellow paper and cut out. Cut within the pencil lines so you don't get any marks and the template doesn't get bigger. Use the glue stick to attach the lady to the card blank.

3 Cut out the individual items of clothing from the template – you need to cut extremely accurately. Referring to the photograph, put the templates onto the appropriate pieces of coloured paper. Keep the tracing paper on the templates to remind you which is the right side. Draw around the templates and cut out.

4 Trace the tree template on page 135 twice. Cut out from green paper and using the marks on the template as a guide, stick onto the main picture, sliding slightly underneath the lady.

5 Start positioning and sticking the clothes onto the main picture. Start from the bottom and work upwards – overskirt, sleeves, hands, cape, and so on.

6 Cut four 5mm (¼in) wide lengths of violet paper. Glue them around the edges of the card to form a border and then cut off the excess.

spring surprise

Lemon yellow, spring green and crisp white – this parchment card is just the thing to brighten up an early spring birthday. This Victorian craft has enjoyed a revival and materials and equipment are available in most craft shops. I have united the old with the new in the form of modern gel pens and traditional parchment to create this delightful card.

you will need

- A5 sheet of light green paper
- Tracing paper
- Pencil
- A5 sheet of plain parchment
- Non-permanent adhesive tape
- Small, sharp scissors
- A5 sheet of white paper
- Small ball embossing tool
- Metal ruler
- Embossing pad
- Daisy tool
- Gel pens in white, lemon and green
- Yellow felt tip pen
- Clear glue
- Scrap piece of coloured paper

timing Parchment craft takes time and patience but the results can be quite beautiful. It's best to practise the techniques on a scrap of parchment paper first.

message The perfect card for a thoughtful greeting.

1 Fold the green sheet of paper in half to create the card blank. Trace or photocopy the design on page 135. Bearing in mind that the design is marked on the reverse side of the card, lay the A5 sheet of parchment over the design, fix in position with non-permanent adhesive tape and mark out the scalloped edge with a pencil.

2 Carefully remove the adhesive tape and use the sharp scissors to cut out the scalloped design.

3 Once again, lay the parchment over the design. If you traced the template, place a piece of white paper underneath the tracing so that you can see the design clearly. Use the embossing tool to mark out the double oval, then use a ruler to mark out the diagonal lines.

4 Place the parchment on the embossing pad. Decorate the oval border between the lines with the daisy tool, pressing the tool firmly into the paper.

continued ▶

5 Working on the reverse side of the parchment, use the embossing tool to score a line down the centre of the card at the edge of the design (line is indicated on design). Score another line 1.5mm (1/16in) away from the first line. This forms the spine of the card.

6 Turn the parchment back to the right side and decorate with gel pens. Colour the daisy petals white, the centres yellow and the stems green. Colour the yellow ribbon using the gel pen and the felt tip pen.

7 Place the card onto a piece of scrap coloured paper (for additional clarity while working). Make four yellow dots at the intersections of the diagonal lines. Decorate around the edge of the card with yellow and green gel pens. Finally, apply glue to the inside of the spine and insert the green folded card.

speckled eggs

A sheet of pale green handmade paper reminiscent of the colour and patterning of wild birds' egg shells was the inspiration for this textured spring greetings card. Egg shapes have been cut from scraps of green and gold paper and embellished with gold outliner, birds' feathers and stars. As this card is not a standard size, you will need to make a matching envelope.

continued ▶

you will need

- Pencil and metal ruler
- Craft knife
- Cutting board
- A3 sheet of textured white card
- A4 sheet of pale green speckled handmade paper
- Glue stick
- Gold outliner
- Tracing paper
- Scissors
- Scraps of gold paper
- Piece of scrap paper
- Gold sparkle embossing powder
- Tweezers
- Gold stars
- A few small feathers

timing Making this card will take you some time but the effect is well worth it.

message A wonderful card to send as an Easter greeting.

1 Measure and cut out a 30 x 15cm (12 x 6in) rectangle of textured white card. Fold in half to create the card blank. Measure out a 13cm (5in) square on the pale green paper and tear out the shape. Glue it centrally on the white card.

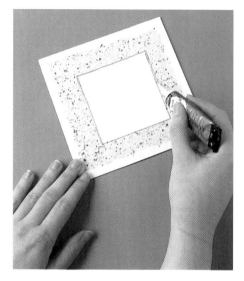

2 Measure and cut out an 8cm (3¼in) square from the textured white card and glue centrally on top of the pale green paper. Decorate the edge of the white card with gold outliner. Leave to harden.

3 To make the eggs, trace the template on page 136 and cut out a number of egg shapes from scraps of speckled green and gold paper. The eggs can be decorated in a number of ways.

4 Make a pattern on the eggs using gold outliner. Lay the eggs on a piece of scrap paper and, before the outliner dries, sprinkle the embossing powder over them. Tip the excess powder back into the pot.

5 To attach gold stars, pick up a star with the tweezers, draw the back of it gently over the glue stick and then place in position on the egg.

6 Once the gold outlined border has hardened, arrange the egg shapes on the card. When you are happy with the arrangement, glue in place. Use glue to attach the feathers and, as a final touch, tiny gold stars to highlight your card.

7 If you wish, make a co-ordinating envelope (see page 15) from pale green speckled handmade paper and decorate it with more eggs.

Attach tags to tiny bunches of flowers.

spice rack

This card not only looks great, it smells wonderful as well. It would look good mounted in a simple wooden frame and hung on the kitchen wall.

you will need

- A4 sheet of buff handmade paper
- A4 sheet of white card
- Spray adhesive
- Set square
- Pencil and metal ruler
- Craft knife
- Cutting board
- A5 sheet of brown paper
- A5 sheet of terracotta honeycomb paper
- A5 sheet of cream textured paper
- Glue stick
- Tracing paper
- Non-permanent adhesive tape
- Clear adhesive
- Selection of interesting shaped herbs and spices

timing Set aside an evening to make this highly effective card.

message Send birthday greetings to your foody friends.

1 Glue the buff handmade paper to the sheet of white card, using spray adhesive. Measure a 25 x 11cm (10 x 4½in) rectangle, cut out and fold in half to form the card blank.

2 Measure a rectangle 10 x 8cm (4 x 3¼in) on the brown paper, a rectangle 9 x 7cm (3½ x 2¾in) on the terracotta honeycomb paper and a rectangle 8 x 6cm (3¼ x 2½in) on the cream paper and cut out. Using the glue stick, glue the rectangles one on top of the other on the front of the card.

3 Trace the template on page 136 onto tracing paper. Place the tracing on the remaining cream paper, fix in position with tape and cut out the basic shape and the nine windows. Glue onto the cream rectangle.

4 Squeeze some clear adhesive into each window and carefully place different herbs or spices into each one. Leave to dry.

A selection of spicy gift tags.

champagne celebration

An explosion of paper streamers and foil stars creates a stunning celebration card. The art of quilling was popular in the Victorian era. Narrow strips of paper were coiled and shaped into intricate patterns and used to decorate picture frames, boxes and even small pieces of furniture. This card and the next one provide two examples of quilling, one traditional and one more modern. Practise the basic techniques first, before you try your hand at creating a masterpiece of your own.

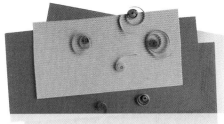

you will need

- A3 sheet of red card
- Pencil and metal ruler
- Set square
- Craft knife
- Cutting board
- A4 sheet of gold card
- A4 sheet of blue ribbed card
- Glue stick
- Tracing paper
- Scissors
- Natural corrugated card
- Quilling streamers in various colours
- Quilling tool
- PVA glue
- Small paint brush
- Foil stars
- Tweezers
- Gold outliner

timing Take a little time over this card for the best results.

message Time to celebrate – send with 18th or 21st birthday greetings.

Festive tags with which to address your gifts.

1 Measure a rectangle, 30 x 15cm (12 x 6in) on the red card. Cut out and fold in half. On the back of the gold card, mark a 12.5 x 12.5cm (5 x 5in) square. Mark out a 2cm (¾in) wide frame and use the craft knife to cut it out.

2 On the blue ribbed card, mark out a 11.5 x 11.5cm (4¼ x 4¼in) square and cut it out. Mark up a 1cm (⅓in) wide frame and cut out with the craft knife. Glue the layers one on top of the other, using a glue stick.

3 Trace the bottle template on page 136 and cut out. Trace around the template on natural corrugated card and cut out. Cut a label from gold card and use the glue stick to attach it to the bottle. Glue the bottle to the bottom right corner of the card.

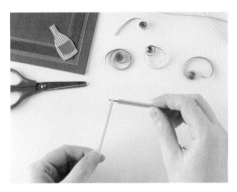

4 To begin quilling you need streamers 15cm (6in) long. Use the quilling tool to curl the ends by threading the streamer into the tool, winding around and then letting go. Repeat to make eight streamers.

5 Put a small blob of PVA glue on a scrap of card. Use the paint brush to apply the glue and carefully place the streamers on the card to create an explosive effect.

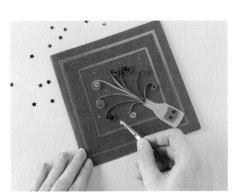

6 When all the streamers are in place, decorate the card with foil stars. Outline the top of the bottle and label with gold outliner.

vase of tulips

This vase of golden tulips makes a card just perfect for Mother's Day. Once you have

mastered the quilling technique, try making different flower and leaf shapes.

you will need

- A5 sheet of yellow textured card
- Pencil and metal ruler
- Set square
- A5 sheet of red card
- Craft knife
- Cutting board
- Glue stick

- A4 sheet of white handmade paper
- Paint brush
- Quilling streamers in brown, yellow and green
- Quilling tool
- Scissors
- PVA glue

timing Quilling is an intricate craft so have plenty of time and patience when making the card.

message The ideal card for Mother's Day – just add a bunch of real tulips as an extra gift for a special person.

1 Create the card base by folding the yellow textured card in half. Measure a rectangle 9 x 7cm (3½ x 2¾in) on the red card and cut out.

2 Using the glue stick, glue the red card onto the yellow card base in a high central position.

3 Measure a rectangle 8 x 6cm (3¼ x 2¼in) on the white handmade paper. Using the paint brush, paint a line of water around the rectangle, thoroughly soaking the paper. Carefully tear it out. Using the glue stick, glue it on top of the red card.

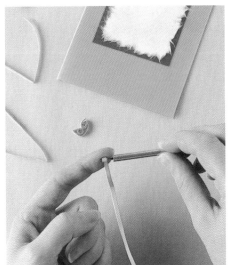

4 To make the flowers, fold a 15cm (6in) length of yellow quilling streamer in half. Using the quilling tool, coil one end of the streamer towards the fold.

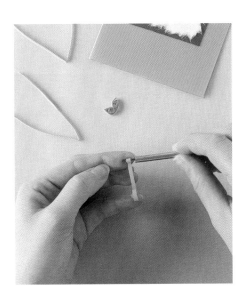

5 Release the coil from the tool, thread in the other end of the streamer and coil up towards the central fold.

continued ▶

Make simple quilled flowers to decorate gift tags.

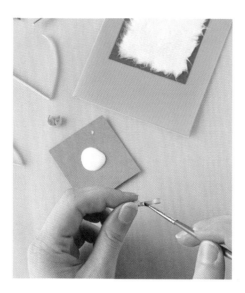

6 Place a small blob of PVA glue on a scrap of card. Allow the coils to unwind slightly, then glue the ends in place near the central fold.

7 Pinch the twin coils into a double teardrop shape to create the tulip flower. You need to make four flowers.

8 Coil three tiny bud shapes from yellow streamers and carefully glue the ends in place. Using the paint brush and PVA glue, stick the flowers and buds in position on the front of the card.

9 Each leaf needs a 15cm (6in) length of green streamer. Wind the streamer tightly around the quilling tool, release the streamer, then pinch into a scroll shape about 1cm (½in) long. Glue the ends in place.

10 The vase is made from three brown 20cm (8in) lengths of quilling streamer. Coil each length tightly around the quilling tool then release and pinch into a large eye shape. Glue the end in place and use PVA glue to attach to the card.

pop-up parrots

Pop-up cards can be quite difficult to make, but this one featuring bright and jolly parrots on a jungle background uses a simple movement.

continued ▶

you will need

- A4 sheets of heavy paper in dark olive green, red, lime green, apple green
- Pencil and metal ruler
- Set square
- Craft knife
- Cutting board
- Glue stick
- 2 A4 sheets of translucent sky blue paper
- Spray adhesive
- A4 sheet of white paper
- Tracing paper
- Scissors
- Yellow gel pen
- Paint brush
- Watercolour paints in yellow, dark and pale green, blue and red
- Black marker pen

  1 Cut a piece of dark olive green heavy paper into a rectangle 24 x 12cm (9½ x 4¾in). Score and fold in half to create the card base. Cut a 10 x 10cm (4 x 4in) square of red heavy paper and stick on the front of the card. Cut a 9 x 9cm (3½ x 3½in) square of blue translucent paper. Using spray adhesive, back this with a square of white paper and, using the glue stick, glue onto the red paper.

timing Pop-up cards take time to make, so set aside an hour or two.

message A great fun greeting for a young child.

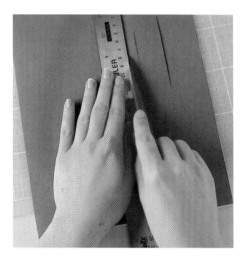

2 Using pencil trace the template on page 137 onto another sheet of translucent blue paper. Apply spray adhesive and attach it to the sheet of white paper and cut along the pencil outlines and cutting lines for the pop-up. Fold in half, with the white paper on the outside.

3 Fold back the first narrow tab and the large outer tab, then flatten down and open up the card.

4 Now pinch and pull these tabs outwards to create the structure of the pop-up. Apply glue to the areas of the white paper that will stick on the card base and glue inside the green card.

5 Using the templates on page 136, trace the foliage onto the various green cards and cut out. Trace and cut out the red flowers.

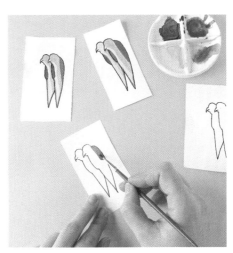

6 Using the glue stick, glue the various items in place inside the card. If any items overhang the sides, simply trim them.

7 Now attach the branch and flowers to the front of the card. Highlight the red flowers used on both the inside and outside of the card with yellow gel pen.

8 Trace the parrot template on page 136 and draw four pairs of parrots. Paint the parrots, copying the colours in the photo above.

9 Highlight and outline the parrots with black marker pen and add the eyes. Carefully cut out the parrots just outside the black outline.

10 Stick three pairs of parrots in position on the inside of the card, on the tabs. Make sure you position them so that the card can close without creasing the parrots.

11 Finally, using the glue stick, stick the fourth set of parrots in position on the front of the card.

ways with colour

projects

pretty daisies

He loves me, he loves me not, he loves me, he loves me not. White daisies with long, fragile stems, layered on lilac, green and white card, create this simply stylish birthday greeting.

you will need

- A5 sheet of lilac card
- Craft knife
- Pencil and metal ruler
- Set square
- Cutting board
- A5 sheet of green card
- A5 sheet of white textured card
- Glue stick
- Yellow watercolour paper
- Watercolour paints in white, green and orange
- Fine paint brush
- Scissors

timing Take your time when making this card and enjoy the painting.

message The spring colours of this card will brighten up a wintry day and bring a little sunshine into someone's home.

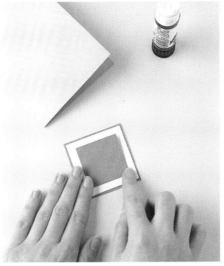

1 Fold the A5 sheet of lilac card in half to create the card blank. Next, create a layered effect by cutting the following: a 6.5 x 6.5cm (2½ x 2½in) square and a 4.5 x 4.5cm (1¼ x 1¼in) square of green card; 6 x 6cm (2¼ x 2¼in) square of white textured card. Layer as shown and glue onto the card base.

2 Paint the flowers on the yellow watercolour paper in groups of three, well spaced apart. Paint the white flowerheads first, followed by the green stems and leaves. It is a good idea to paint a few and choose the best one for your card. Spares can be used as gift tags.

Use any leftover daisies to decorate some gift tags.

3 When the white paint has dried, add orange centres to the daisies with a small dot of paint. Leave to dry.

4 When dry, use the set square and pencil to measure squares 4 x 4cm (1½ x 1½in) around the flowers and carefully cut out. Glue in place on the front of the card.

oriental flowers

Simply beautiful. The exquisite marble inlay work which decorates the Taj Mahal in India inspired this lovely card. You might want to create your own picture of flowers rather than use the template.

you will need

- A5 sheet of white textured paper
- Pencil and metal ruler
- Craft knife
- Cutting board
- Tracing paper
- Gel pens in gold, green, pale blue and pink

 timing Once the picture is traced this card takes very little time to make.

 message This gentle card could be used to convey a message of sympathy.

1 Cut a 13.5 x 15cm (5¼ x 6in) piece from the sheet of white textured paper. Measure and mark the centre. Score the centre line and fold in half.

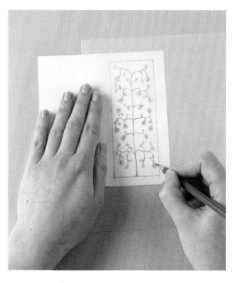

2 Open the card. Trace the template on page 138. Place the traced pattern over the front of the card and trace over the pattern again in pencil, to leave an impression in the textured paper.

3 Use the gold gel pen to create the border then, following the traced pattern, go over the stem, branches, leaves and flowers.

4 Looking closely at the photograph of the finished card, use the pink, green and blue pens to colour in the flowers and leaves.

Some freehand gilded swirls, petals and leaves turn plain gift tags into something quite special.

Christmas crib

I found this beautiful paper in a gift shop. It seems to change colour from spangled gold to peach to red, rather like an amazing sunset. I thought it made the ideal backdrop for a special Christmas card. To ring the changes make the card with a midnight blue sky or a golden yellow dawn.

you will need

- Suitable wrapping paper
- Pencil and metal ruler
- Set square
- Craft knife
- Cutting board
- Glue stick
- A5 sheet of white paper
- Tracing paper
- Non-permanent adhesive tape
- A5 sheet of stiff card, for template
- Scissors
- A5 sheet of black card
- Gold pen
- Gold outliner

timing Tracing the picture takes time, so settle down with a cup of tea to make this card.

message A lovely Christmas card to take pride of place on the mantelpiece.

1 Cut the wrapping paper to A5 size. Use the glue stick to attach the A5 sheet of white paper to the reverse side of the wrapping paper. Fold in half. This is your card blank.

2 To create the skyline, use a pencil and tracing paper to trace the template on page 138. Lightly stick the tracing paper template to a piece of stiff card and cut around the top and bottom outlines. Position this card template 1.5cm (¾in) from the bottom edge of the black card. Fix in position with non-permanent adhesive tape, then draw around the top and bottom outlines with a gold pen.

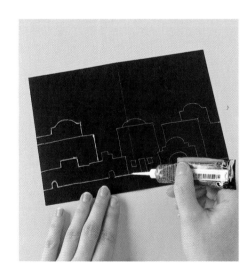

3 Fill in the rest of the detail with gold pen, then go over the lines with the gold outliner. You may need to practise a few lines and curves on a spare piece of paper before you begin to draw over the gold lines. Fill in all the decorative details, including the crib. Leave to dry.

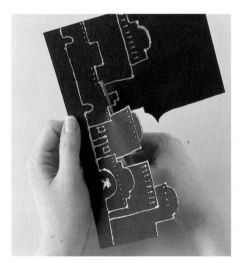

4 Once the gold outlines are dry, use scissors to cut out the picture along the top outline. Take care not to cut off the gold outliner.

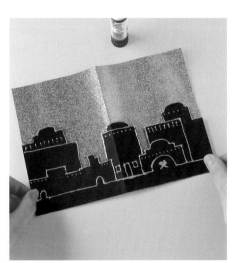

5 Glue the black cut-out onto the 'sky'. Add the star of Bethlehem above the stable to complete the card.

glitz and glamour

To make a change from robins and Christmas trees, here silver birds and glitter glue are used to decorate this festive party card. The delicate stencilled bird can be printed on a variety of coloured tissue papers and glued onto silver card for a magical effect. You might like to mass-produce these cards as they are so quick and easy to make.

you will need

- Tracing paper
- Pencil and metal ruler
- Spray adhesive
- A4 sheet of thin card
- Craft knife
- Cutting board
- Silver acrylic paint

- Saucer
- Sponge
- Tissue paper
- A5 sheet of silver card
- Glue stick
- Green glitter glue
- Foil stars and glittery strips

timing Once set up, this card takes no time at all to make. A good card to mass produce.

message Suitable as a party invitation or seasonal greeting.

1 Trace the bird template on page 138. Spray a thin layer of spray adhesive onto the back of the tracing and attach it to the thin card. Use a craft knife to cut out a stencil from the card.

2 Pour a small quantity of silver paint onto the saucer and dip the sponge in it (do not put too much paint onto the sponge). Lay the stencil on the tissue paper and stencil silver birds onto it, dabbing with the sponge. Leave to dry.

3 Cut a piece of silver card 21 x 11cm (8½ x 4¼in). Fold in half to form the basic card. Use the ruler and pencil to draw a 7.5cm (3in) square around the motif and carefully cut it out. Use the glue stick to attach it centrally on the card.

4 Draw a glitter glue border around the design. Decorate the card with stars and glittery strips. It is easiest to pick up each strip or star with tweezers, pass it over the glue stick and then position on the card.

Experiment with different coloured papers and decorative elements.

robin red breast

Stencilling is an excellent technique to use when you need to make lots of greetings cards. Commercially produced stencils are available from art and craft shops, but they are also fairly simple to make yourself and once you have the stencil, prints are quick to make.

Put your stencil to good use and make an interesting selection of cards.

you will need

- Pencil and metal ruler
- Tracing paper
- Glue stick
- Thin card
- Craft knife
- Cutting board
- Gold acrylic paint
- Saucer

- Sponge
- Black tissue paper
- Red glitter glue
- Black felt tip pen
- A5 sheet of cream textured card
- Scissors
- Gold foil
- A5 sheet of red textured paper

timing This card is very quick to do and is great for children to make. A good card to mass produce.

message This cute little robin will send a delightful seasonal message to family and friends at Christmas. You could also create your own layered look in different colours.

1 Using a pencil and tracing paper, trace the robin template on page 139. Use the glue stick to attach it to the thin card. Cut out the stencil carefully with a craft knife. It is a good idea to prepare two or three stencils, especially if you want to make a lot of cards.

2 Pour a little gold paint onto a saucer and press the sponge into the paint Do not use too much paint. Spread the black tissue paper out, hold the stencil firmly in place and dab the sponge onto the stencil. You might want to stencil more robins than you will need and use the best prints.

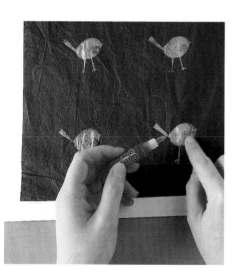

3 Once the gold paint is dry, dab the red glitter glue onto the robin's breast. Make a black dot for its eye with felt tip pen. Now you are ready to put the card together.

4 Make a card base by folding the cream card in half. As this card has a naive feel to it, the layers are cut approximately to shape. The first layer is a rectangle of gold foil approximately 7.5 x 9.5cm (3 x 3¾in), glued onto the cream card. Glue in a high central position on the card base.

5 The second layer is a rectangle approximately 6.5 x 7.5cm (2¾ x 3in) cut from red textured paper. Glue it on top of the gold. Finally, cut out a rectangle around the robin motif, approximately 5 x 6cm (2 x 2½in) and glue it on top of the red paper.

spring greeting

found this delightful stamp at my local art and craft shop and was inspired to create an Easter card. I chose yellow and green colours to remind me of spring daffodils and the mother duck and her ducklings sit pretty and proud.

you will need

- A5 sheet of brown speckled card
- Duck stamp
- Felt tip pens in yellow, orange and brown
- A4 sheet of white card
- Pencil and metal ruler
- Set square
- Craft knife
- Cutting board
- Sheet of yellow and green opaque paper
- Glue stick
- White paper
- Green gel pen
- Yellow fabric paint

timing Set aside an hour when making this card and be sure to let the various elements dry before posting.

message Send a springtime greeting to friends with this bright card.

1 Create the card base by folding the A5 sheet of brown card in half. Take the stamp and colour the duck brown, her feet, beak and the ducklings' beaks orange and the ducklings yellow.

2 Print the picture onto white card. It is a good idea to print a number of pictures and use the best one. Hold the stamp very firmly and lift it straight off the paper so that the image does not blur.

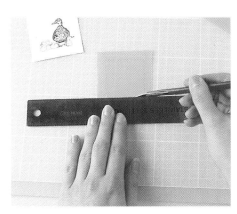

3 Cut out the duck family, leaving a 1cm (½in) border all around the print. Cut out a 6.5cm (2¾in) square of yellow opaque paper and then use the craft knife to cut out a central window 4.5cm (1¾in) square. Glue onto the duck picture to create a border.

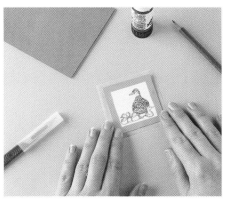

4 Use a glue stick to attach this centrally to a 7.5 x 7.5cm (3 x 3in) square of green opaque paper and finally attach this to a slightly larger piece of white paper. Use a glue stick to attach the layered picture to the front of the card in a high central position.

5 Use the green gel pen to draw a neat line of leaves around the yellow card border, leaving small spaces between the leaves.

6 Finally, add yellow fabric paint dots between the green leaves. Allow to dry.

Christmas candle

This glittery card shows how effective a repeat pattern can be. You could use this idea to create other card designs, such as Christmas trees, stars or holly leaves.

you will need

- **A4 sheet** of white textured card
- **Pencil and metal** ruler
- **Set square**
- **Craft knife**
- **Cutting board**
- **Candle stamp**
- **Embossing stamp** pad
- **Scrap paper**
- **Red embossing** powder
- **Tweezers or metal** tongs
- **Precision heat tool**
- **Gold glitter** embossing powder
- **A5 sheet of red** card
- **Glue stick**

timing This card is very simple to make, you could make a number of cards in an evening.

 message A sophisticated festive greeting.

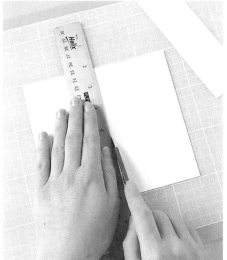

1 Mark out a rectangle 16 x 15cm (6¼ x 6in) in pencil on the white card, then cut out with the craft knife and metal ruler. With the longest edge at the top, score down the centre and fold. This is your card blank.

2 On the remaining white textured card, stamp a row of candles. You will barely be able to see the design as the ink is clear. Stamp more images than you need, as some may not be perfect.

3 Working quickly, fold a sheet of scrap paper in half, then open it out. Holding the stamped card over the scrap paper, sprinkle over the red embossing powder (you need to do this before the ink dries). Shake the excess powder back onto the paper, then tip it back into the pot.

4 Holding the stamped card with tweezers or tongs, heat the embossing powder with the heat tool (see page 12) until melted. Mark a pencil rectangle 5 x 3.5cm (2 x 1¼in) around each stamp, keeping the design central, and cut out.

continued ▶

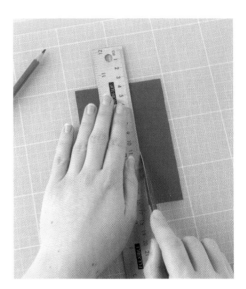

5 Sprinkle gold glitter embossing powder onto the scrap paper. Working quickly, press each edge of the design into the side of the embossing stamp pad (this is where there is most ink).

6 Dip the edges of the card rectangle into the gold powder. Melt with the heat tool as before.

7 Measure out a rectangle 12 x 5.5cm (4¾ x 2¼in) on the sheet of red card and cut out.

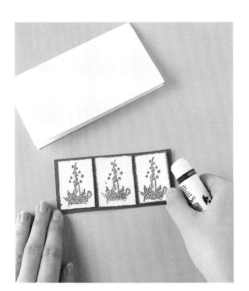

8 Glue three candle images onto the red card, then glue the red rectangle onto the white card blank.

Look around for other interesting stamps to use for cards and gift tags.

dolphin display

Leaping dolphins always make a fine picture. Glass paint works well on acetate, creating a stained-glass effect. It can take up to 24 hours to dry so be sure to leave enough time to create this card.

continued ▶

you will need

- A5 sheet of white textured card
- Pencil and metal ruler
- Set square
- Pair of compasses
- Cutting board
- Craft knife
- A5 sheet of red paper
- Double-sided adhesive tape
- Tracing paper
- Black marker pen
- Acetate
- Non-permanent adhesive tape
- Glass paints in white, black, blue and green
- Palette
- Paint brush

timing Glass painting takes time, so this card is best made over a weekend to give the paint time to dry thoroughly.

message A good all-purpose greetings card. Send to friends about to go on holiday or as a birthday greeting.

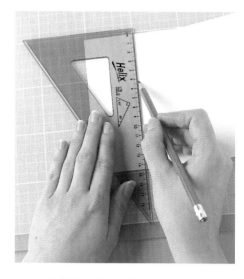

1 Fold the sheet of A5 paper in half to make the card blank. To create the circular window, open the card blank. The left-hand inside leaf of the card should measure 10.5cm (4¼in) across. Divide this in half and you have 5.25cm (2⅛in). Lightly rule a line down the card to mark the centre. Next, lie the set square down the ruled line and make a mark 5.25cm (2⅛in) down from the top of the card. This is the centre of the circle.

2 Place the point of the compasses on the centre mark and draw a circle with a 3.5cm (1⅜in) radius.

3 Place the card on the cutting board and carefully cut out the circle using the craft knife. This is not easy, so take your time.

4 Cut a 10cm (4in) square from the red paper. Draw two diagonal pencil lines across the square to find the centre point, then draw a circle with a 3cm (1¼in) radius and, as in step 3, cut it out. Using double-sided tape, stick the red card inside the white card, to form a red border around the window. Before fixing firmly in place, look from the front of the card to ensure the red circle is displayed evenly.

5 Trace the dolphin template on page 139. Place this beneath the acetate and hold in place with non-permanent tape. Use a marker pen to trace the picture onto the acetate.

6 Colour in the dolphins with glass paint. Be sure not to go over the marker pen lines. You will need to leave the picture until quite dry – this may take several hours.

Keep the shapes simple when creating your own designs.

7 Once the paint has dried, you can put the card together. Use double-sided tape to attach the dolphin painting so that it is centred within the window.

poppy field

Whether you are a beginner or an expert, creating stained-glass effect cards can be highly rewarding. I have chosen bright red poppies set against a background of green fields and a blue sky to decorate this versatile card.

you will need

- Tracing paper
- Pencil and metal ruler
- Acetate
- Non-permanent adhesive tape
- Black marker pen
- Glass paints in red, green and blue
- Paint brush
- A5 sheet of white textured card
- Set square
- A5 sheet of red card
- Craft knife
- Cutting board
- Double-sided adhesive tape

timing Although this card is very simple, it can't be made in a rush as the painting must be done neatly and the paint takes some time to dry.

message This could be a birthday card or sent as a Valentine, or maybe in memory of a summer picnic in the country.

1 Trace the template on page 139. Place the template beneath the acetate and hold in place with non-permanent tape. Use the marker pen to trace the template onto the acetate.

2 Use the glass paints to colour in the poppies and the background, then leave to dry for several hours.

3 Fold the A5 sheet of white card in half to form the card blank. Using the ruler, set square and pencil, measure a square of red card 1cm (½in) wider and deeper than the picture. Draw a border 5mm (¼in) inside the square and cut out the central area to form a picture frame.

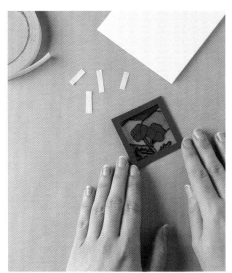

4 When the paints are dry, use double-sided tape to attach the red frame to the acetate, then attach this with double-sided tape in a high central position on the card blank.

projects

cat on the mat

Brown paper, fabric scraps and a white felt cat with glowing green glitter glue eyes create this friendly greetings card. I have used squares of small print patchwork fabric to create a homely look. Use whatever fabric scraps you have to hand and simple felt animal shapes to create your own designs.

Scraps of fabric and sequins are useful when creating cards and tags.

you will need

- A5 sheet of mottled beige paper
- Metal ruler
- Craft knife
- Cutting board
- Blue fabric, 8.5 x 8.5cm (3¾ x 3¾in)
- Patterned fabric, 7.5 x 7.5cm (3 x 3in)
- Dotted fabric, 6 x 6cm (2½ x 2½in)
- Spray adhesive
- Scissors
- Tracing paper
- Pencil
- White felt
- Embroidery scissors
- White cotton thread
- Needle
- PVA glue
- Green glitter glue

timing Once you have cut out the shapes, it won't take long to make this card as all the elements are glued into place.

message A good card to send to friends settling into a new home.

1 Score and fold the sheet of mottled beige paper in half to create the card blank.

2 Prepare the fabric by spraying the back of the squares with spray adhesive. Attach the blue piece of fabric to the card blank in an upper central position. Place the patterned fabric square centrally on top of the blue fabric and the dotted fabric square on top of that.

3 Trace the template on page 140 and cut out. Draw around the template onto the white felt and use embroidery scissors to cut out the cat shape.

4 The cat's whiskers are created using white cotton thread. Thread the needle and simply push it through the felt, pulling so that approximately 1cm (½in) of thread pokes out one side. Trim the other side so that it is even. Repeat three times.

5 Use PVA glue to stick the cat centrally on to the layered fabric. Finally, give the cat two green eyes by squeezing tiny green glitter glue dots on to the cat's face.

Christmas pudding

An embroidered motif on white silk on a white and gold card base makes up this

extra special card with which to send Christmas greetings.

you will need

- A5 sheet of textured white card
- Pencil and metal ruler
- Craft knife
- Cutting board
- White paper with gold speckles
- Tracing paper
- Scissors
- Scrap paper
- Gold glitter embossing powder
- Embossing pad
- Precision heat tool
- Glue stick
- Gold pen
- White silk, 8 x 8cm (3¼ x 3¼in)
- Thin polyester wadding, 8 x 8cm (3¼ x 3¼in)
- Pins
- Embroidery thread in golden yellow, rich brown, green and red
- Needle
- Double-sided tape

timing Completing the embroidery for this card will take a little time but the finished product will be worth it.

message A really special seasonal greeting to send to a best friend or favourite relative.

1 Fold the card in half. Measure in 3cm (1¼in) from each side and from the top and draw a 4.5cm (1¾in) square. Use a craft knife to cut out the square.

2 Trace the border template on page 139. Position on the white and gold paper and cut out the centre square with a craft knife. Cut out the shape with scissors.

3 Fold the scrap paper in half, open out and tip the embossing powder onto it. Press the edges of the border into the pad, then dip into the powder. Use the heat tool (see page 12) to fix.

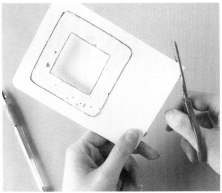

4 Glue this frame onto the card base. Draw a thin border around the central square with the gold pen. Carefully round the corners of the card base.

5 Pin the silk square to the wadding. Embroider a line of backstitch in yellow. Embroider the outline of the pudding in brown thread, then fill in the centre. Embroider the leaves in green and the holly berries in red. An outline of the pudding shape is included on page 139.

6 Using double-sided tape, position the embroidered picture behind the window and stick it in place.

scented lavender

Lavender, muslin and a little simple embroidery set on handmade paper makes the perfect birthday card. Harvesting aromatic lavender flowers is a seasonal pastime I look forward to every year. Pick them in the morning when the dew has dried. Hang bunches in a shady, airy spot for a few weeks. Packed away in paper bags, lavender will hold its fragrance for many years.

you will need

- Muslin, 22 x 16cm (8½ x 6½in)
- Scissors
- Needle
- White thread
- Small handful of lavender
- Teaspoon
- Lavender coloured narrow ribbon

- Embroidery threads in green and lavender
- A5 sheet of white patterned paper
- Glue stick
- Blue handmade paper, 8 x 11cm (3¼ x 4½in) with torn edges
- PVA glue
- Paint brush

timing A lavender harvest, embroidery and a little crafting make this a more time-consuming card but the result is a memory which will last for years.

message Send to a friend who needs a little cheering up.

1 Fold the muslin in half. The fold will become the upper edge of the bag.

2 Fold in half again the other way. Keeping the folded edge at the top, bring the raw edges together and sew a line of running stitch from top to bottom on the longest side. (The stitching is best done in white thread – I've used blue here so that it can be clearly seen.)

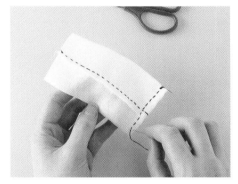

3 Open the partly-made bag to make the seam you have just sewn form the centre back of the bag. Sew a seam across the bottom of the bag. Turn the bag right side out.

4 Fill loosely with lavender. Tie a ribbon bow tightly around the top to hold it in place.

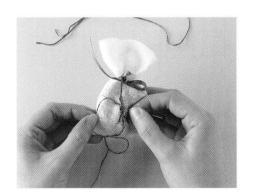

5 Neatly sew violet French knots and green backstitch stems to the bag to make a bunch of lavender (see pattern on page 140).

6 To make the card base, fold the sheet of A5 white patterned card in half. Use the glue stick to centrally attach a torn piece of lavender blue handmade paper. Use PVA glue to attach the lavender bag (use just a little glue so that the bag can be detached from the card and used to scent a drawer or wardrobe).

woven ribbon

This woven ribbon heart in delicate creams, pinks and greens is bordered with a cotton lace frill and set in heavy watercolour paper. Ribbon weaving was a popular pastime amongst the nimble-fingered middle classes of Victorian and Regency England. Modern spray adhesives and the wide range of ribbons available make this an extremely accessible hobby.

you will need

- A5 sheet of pink card
- Pencil and metal ruler
- Set square
- Craft knife
- Cutting board
- Sheet of light-weight paper
- Spray adhesive
- Selection of narrow ribbons in pink, green and cream

- Scissors
- Heavy watercolour paper
- Tracing paper
- 35cm (14in) length of narrow cotton lace
- Glue stick
- Needle
- White thread

timing The craft of ribbon weaving requires patience and time, so set aside a few hours of solitude to make this pretty greetings card.

message A wonderful birthday card or romantic Valentine.

1 The card blank is made from pink card. Use the ruler, set square and pencil to mark up a rectangular shape 10.5 x 15cm (4¼ x 6in). Cut out and fold in half.

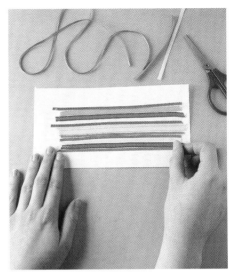

2 Next take a sheet of lightweight paper and spray a 20 x 10cm (8 x 4in) area with spray adhesive. Allow it to become tacky. Place 15cm (6in) lengths of ribbon, one beside the other, across the paper to a depth of 9cm (3½in).

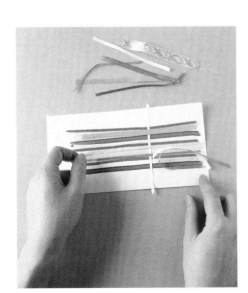

3 Lift up every other length of ribbon, starting with the second strip, and fold it back. Place a length of ribbon vertically then lie the horizontal ribbons back in place.

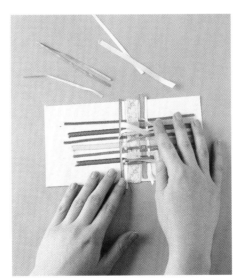

4 Now lift up every other length of ribbon, this time starting with the first strip, and repeat the process with another vertical length of ribbon. Continue until you have covered an area at least 9cm (3½in) square.

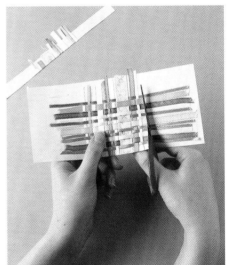

5 When you have made a woven square of ribbon, press the ribbons down firmly on the card so they don't lift up, then trim the card to a square 9 x 9cm (3½ x 3½in).

continued ▶

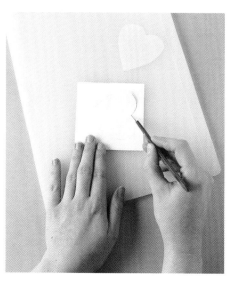

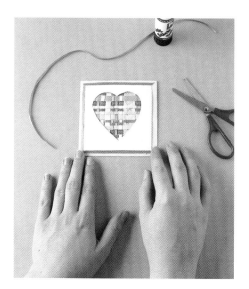

6 Cut a 9 x 9cm (3½ x 3½in) square of watercolour paper. Trace the heart template on page 140 and cut it out. Place the heart shape centrally on the square of watercolour paper and draw around it.

7 Cut out the heart shape using the craft knife.

8 Glue the square of ribbon weaving centrally onto the card blank and glue the heart frame on top of that. Glue a dusky pink ribbon border to the watercolour paper.

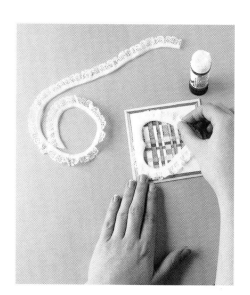

9 Finally, sew a running stitch along the length of lace, gently pull the thread to gather up the lace and attach as a border around the ribbon heart with the glue stick.

Use any excess woven ribbon to create interesting gift tags.

card for cooks

This unusual card uses a variety of materials – gingham fabric, beads, modelling clay and craft foil – all of the useful bits and pieces that you will have stashed away in your card-making box!

continued ▶

you will need

- A5 sheet of turquoise card
- Pencil and metal ruler
- Red gingham fabric
- Fabric scissors
- Spray adhesive
- A5 sheet of white textured card
- Paper scissors
- Set square
- Glue stick
- Scrap of thin craft wood (or beige card)

- Emery board
- Small sheet of craft foil
- Pen
- Modelling clay in light brown
- Two small red beads
- Tracing paper
- Pin
- Scrap of white fabric
- Red cord

timing Rolling out pastry takes time and so this card will take you a while to make, but have fun!

message Send to a young home baker.

1 Fold the turquoise card in half to make the card blank. Measure and cut out a piece of red gingham fabric 8.5 x 13cm (3½ x 5in). Coat the back with spray adhesive and stick centrally on the card.

2 Measure and cut out a 6.5 x 6cm (2¾ x 2½in) piece of white textured card and stick onto the gingham in a high central position using the glue stick.

3 Cut a 2.5 x 4cm (1 x 1½in) piece of craft wood, round the corners with an emery board and glue into position on the white card. Cut out a 2.5 x 3cm (1 x 1¼in) piece of craft foil, rounding the corners. Make an impression around the edge of the foil 'tray' with a pen. Glue in position with the glue stick.

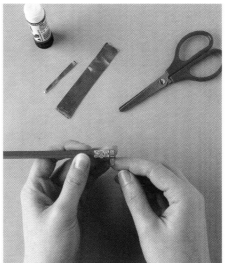

4 Wind a short length of 5mm (¼in) wide craft foil around the end of a pencil to make a cookie cutter shape. Glue the ends together.

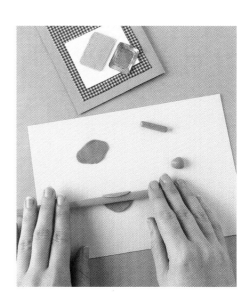

5 Work a small ball of modelling clay between your hands to soften it. Make a rolling pin shape and roll out two small balls of clay (use the body of a smooth pen as a miniature rolling pin).

6 Cut out five biscuit shapes from one round of clay. Using the end of a pencil with the eraser removed, make impressions in the second round of clay. Bake the clay according to the manufacturer's instructions.

7 When baked and cooled, attach the clay to the card using the glue stick. Glue a red bead to each end of the rolling pin and then glue the rolling pin to the card. Glue on the cookie cutter.

8 Trace the apron template from page 141 and cut out. Pin the template to a scrap of white fabric and cut out. Cut out a small pocket shape from gingham.

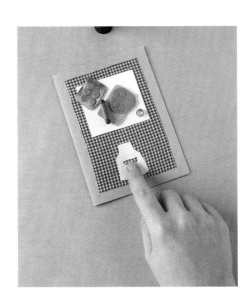

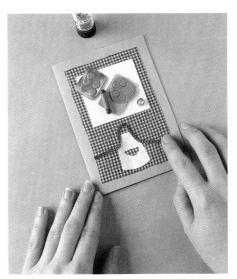

9 Spray the back of the apron with spray adhesive and attach to the card. Attach the pocket with glue stick.

10 Cut an 11cm (4½in) length of red cord or ribbon to form the apron strings and glue in place.

memories of India

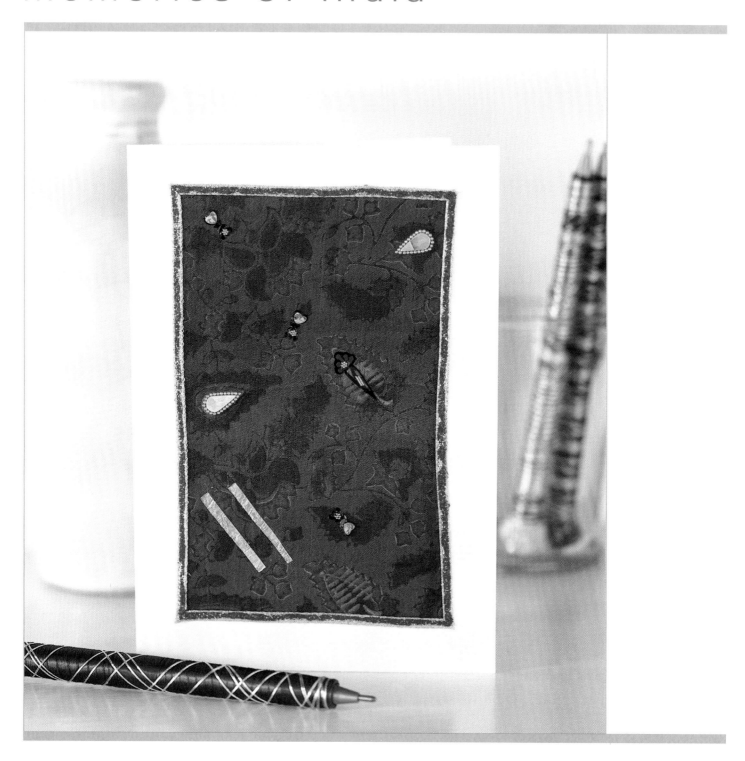

This picture made from richly patterned fabric, decorated gold thread and gilded mirrors was inspired by the richness of colour worn by the talented craftsmen and women who live in the desert state of Rajasthan, in the north-west of India. The silk used here comes from a scarf my grandmother used to wear, now damaged by age and use.

you will need

- A5 sheet of white textured card
- Patterned silk fabric
- Fabric scissors
- Spray adhesive
- A4 sheet of lightweight white paper
- Light coloured felt tip pen

- Set square
- Scissors
- Glue stick
- Narrow gold ribbon
- Bindis or sequins for decoration
- Gold foil
- Pink glitter glue

timing Once you have collected all the materials together this card should not take too long to produce.

message Good as a notelet, birthday greeting or thank-you card.

A hint of India is created in these gift tags with silks, bindis and gold foil.

1 Fold the A5 sheet of textured card in half to create the card blank. Cut a rectangle of silk slightly larger than the card front and use spray adhesive to attach it to a sheet of lightweight white paper.

2 Using a light coloured felt tip pen and a set square, measure out a rectangle 8 x 12cm (3¼ x 4¾in) on the layered fabric and paper.

3 Using sharp scissors, cut out the rectangle of paper and silk. Apply glue to the paper and attach it centrally to the card blank.

4 Your card is now ready for decoration. Glue a border of narrow gold ribbon around the fabric, carefully mitring the edges with sharp scissors.

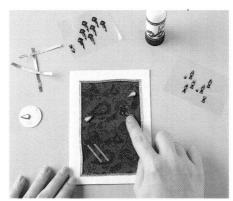

5 Use bindis or sequins and snippets of gold foil to embellish the silk. Attach them with the glue stick.

6 Finally squeeze a line of pink glitter glue along the ribbon border. Leave the glitter glue to dry overnight. You might like to decorate an envelope with a silk border for dramatic effect.

cross-stitch greeting

*Tiny cross-stitch samplers
to send to friends.*

This card, carrying a romantic message in counted cross stitch, was created to send a message of future happiness to a newly engaged couple. Cross stitch can be used to sew simple messages for Mother's Day, weddings and special birthdays.

you will need

- Pencil and metal ruler
- A5 sheet of white textured card
- Craft knife
- Cutting board
- Sewing needle
- Embroidery thread in blue
- Scissors
- Cross-stitch fabric, 8 x 8cm (3¼ x 3¼in)
- Glue stick
- A5 sheet of blue handmade paper

timing This stitched card takes time to complete but the end result is a gift which the happy couple can frame and save forever.

message Send this card for an engagement or wedding or as a housewarming gift.

1 Begin by creating the card blank. Using the ruler and pencil, mark out a rectangle 21 x 10.5cm (8½ x 4¼in) on the white textured card. Cut out and fold in half to create the card blank.

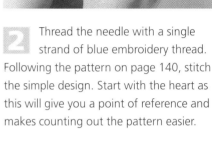

2 Thread the needle with a single strand of blue embroidery thread. Following the pattern on page 140, stitch the simple design. Start with the heart as this will give you a point of reference and makes counting out the pattern easier.

3 Stitch the house and the remainder of the pattern, completing the design with two initials of your choice.

4 Once you have completed the cross-stitch picture, carefully count out a frame around the cross stitch measuring 5 squares on each side. Cut it out.

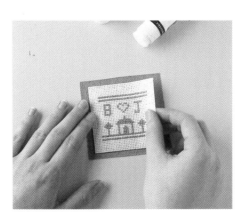

5 Use a glue stick to attach the embroidered fabric centrally to a 9 x 9cm (3½ x 3½in) square of blue handmade paper.

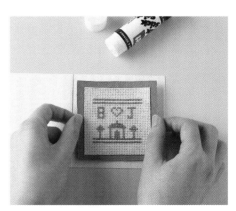

6 Use the glue stick to attach the framed cross stitch to the card blank. You may want to make a matching envelope in blue handmade paper to complete this delightful card.

harvest landscape

The art of painting on silk is used to create original works for friends and relatives to treasure.

I have included patterns for two silk painting cards – see the next project for a different image. This

country harvest scene shows rolling hills, fields and hedges with a copse of trees on the horizon.

you will need

- White silk, 15 x 15cm (6 x 6in)
- Scissors
- Frame, approx. 15 x 15cm (6 x 6in)
- Masking tape
- Black marker pen
- Tracing paper
- Silk paint outliner in gold

- Silk paints in two shades of green, yellow, blue, orange and brown
- Palette
- Paint brush
- A5 sheet of buff coloured speckled card
- Spray adhesive

timing Silk painting takes a while to set up and the outliners need time to dry so set aside an evening for this card. Once you have set up your equipment you might want to create a few designs of your own to decorate future cards.

message This versatile card can be used to send birthday greetings, as a thank-you card or simply to send a thoughtful message to a friend.

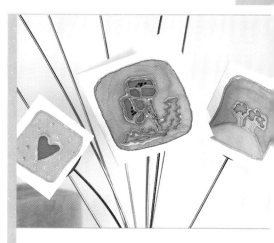

Experiment with silk paints and use the results to make gift tags.

1 Stretch the white silk across the frame. Use masking tape to secure the fabric to the frame. This will hold the fabric taut while you paint.

2 Using a black marker pen, trace the harvest scene from the template on page 141. Place this beneath the silk. Use the gold outliner to trace the pattern onto the silk. Leave to dry. You may want to outline two or three copies of the picture and use the best one for your card.

3 Once the outliner is dry, your picture is ready to colour in. Carefully paint in each colour. You will need the smallest quantity of silk paint on a clean brush as the fabric dye spreads rapidly across the cloth.

4 To create a deeper hue, paint on a second layer of colour, for example on the greenery of the trees and hedges or to create a deeper yellow.

5 When the painting is dry, use scissors to carefully cut it out along the gold outer border.

6 Fold the sheet of card in half to form the card blank. Use spray adhesive to attach the picture to the card.

underwater scene

This magical **underwater scene** in sea greens and blues is bordered with glitter gold and set on a

deep blue card. I hope you will find the design inspirational and go on to create your own designs

in this highly versatile medium.

you will need

- White silk, 15 x 15cm (6 x 6in)
- Scissors
- Frame, approx. 15 x 15 cm (6 x 6in)
- Masking tape
- Black marker pen
- Tracing paper
- Silk paint outliner in gold

- Silk paints in blue, green, yellow, red and brown
- Paint brush
- Palette
- A5 sheet of blue card
- Spray adhesive
- Gold glitter glue

timing Silk painting takes a while to set up and the outliner needs time to dry so set aside an evening for making this card. Once you have set up your painting equipment you might like to create a few designs of your own with which to decorate other cards.

message This versatile card can be used to send birthday greetings or simply a thoughtful message to a friend.

1 Stretch the white silk across the frame. Use masking tape to secure the fabric to the back of the frame.

2 Using a black marker pen, trace the underwater scene from the template on page 141. Place this beneath the silk. Use the gold outliner to trace the pattern onto the silk. Leave to dry. You may want to outline two or three copies of the picture and use the best one for your card.

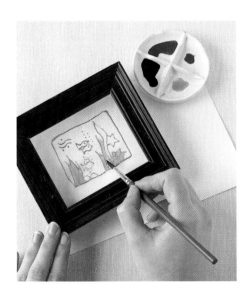

3 Once the outliner is dry you will be able to paint in the colours. You will need the smallest quantity of silk paint on a clean brush as the fabric dye spreads rapidly across the cloth. When the picture is completed, leave to dry.

4 Fold the blue card in half to form the card blank. Cut your silk painting to size following the outer gold border. Coat the back with spray adhesive and when it becomes tacky, place the painting centrally on the upper part of the card.

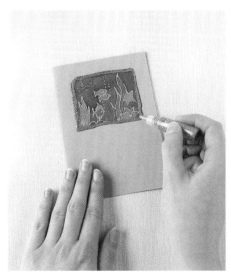

5 Use gold glitter glue to create a border and once the glue has set, you will have a silk painted original to sign and send to a friend.

projects

welcome little stranger

What better way to share the joy of a new baby with grandparents and special friends? I used a computer to scan in the photograph, trimmed the picture and printed off a number of copies.

you will need

- White handmade paper, 23 x 11.5cm (9 x 4½in)
- Pencil and metal ruler
- Craft knife
- Cutting board
- Glue stick
- White textured card, 10 x 10cm (4 x 4in)
- Pale pink heavy textured card, 9 x 9cm (3½ x 3½in)
- Tracing paper
- Scissors
- Flower punch
- Silver pen
- Photograph of the baby

timing A little technical know-how, a touch of artistic talent and a little time will make this delightful card.

message Send to faraway grandparents and special friends to announce the new arrival.

1 Score and fold the piece of white handmade paper in half to create the card blank. Next glue the square of white textured card in a central position on the card base.

2 The image surround is cut from a square of pale pink textured card. Trace the template on page 141 or create a shape suitable for your photograph. Cut it out by first cutting a cross in the centre of the oval with a craft knife and then cutting around the oval with scissors.

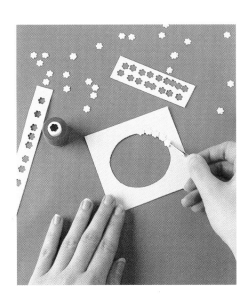

3 Create a decorative frame by using the punch to cut out flowers from card offcuts. Use a glue stick to attach them around the oval shape. Mark a small silver dot in the centre of each flower.

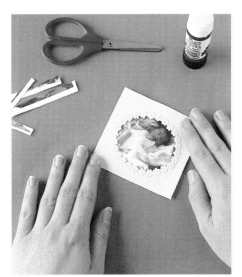

4 Position the decorated frame centrally over the photograph and glue firmly in place.

5 Glue the framed photograph centrally on the card blank and decorate with a silver border and a flower on each corner.

photo frame

This elegant card comprises three-dimensional flowers on a white textured paper

base. It's a wonderful gift and a greeting all-in-one.

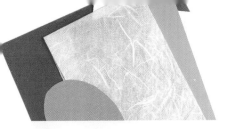

you will need

- 2 A5 sheets of slightly textured white paper
- Pencil and metal ruler
- Craft knife
- Cutting board
- Tracing paper
- Scissors
- White mulberry paper
- Spray adhesive
- Glue stick
- A5 sheet of green paper
- A5 sheet of red paper
- Piece of thick card

timing A very quick card to make – what takes the time is choosing which photograph to enclose.

message A great card to send as a greeting to a friend, particularly if the photograph holds special memories for you both.

1   Fold a sheet of A5 paper in half to create the blank. Trace and cut out the oval template on page 141, position centrally on the card and draw around it. Cut a cross in the oval with a craft knife and then cut around the oval with scissors.

2   Cut the sheet of mulberry paper to a rectangle 23 x 17cm (9 x 6¾in). Coat with spray adhesive and place the card blank on top of it. Mitre the corners, then fold over the overhanging sides and stick down.

3   Using the craft knife, cut a small oval out of the centre, then cut tabs in the remaining overhanging paper, turn in and stick down on the inside of the card.

4   Take the second sheet of A5 paper and trim 5mm (¼in) off all sides. Fold in half. Apply glue stick all over the paper apart from the top of the left-hand side, as this is where the photograph is inserted. Stick the white paper inside the mulberry paper card.

5   Trace the flower and leaf templates on page 141. Cut out eight leaves from green paper. Glue them in place as shown. To make the flowers, cut out four circles from red paper. Make a snip from the edge to the centre and twist the paper to make a shallow cone shape.

6   Glue the flowers to hold their shape. Glue one red cone in each corner of the card, then flatten the cones to make flower shapes – it is easiest to place a piece of thick card over the flowers and then press down. Trim your chosen photograph if necessary and insert.

romantic red rose

This is the perfect Valentine. Layers of handmade paper and a pressed rose create this deeply romantic card. You might be inspired to press other flowers, for example to create a pressed pansy birthday card. Flower presses are available from craft shops but you can also layer the flowers between cartridge paper, place inside a heavy book and place a weight on top of the book.

you will need

- Pencil and metal ruler
- A3 sheet of white handmade paper
- Set square
- Scissors
- A4 sheet of pink handmade paper
- Glue stick
- A5 sheet of cream textured card
- Pressed rose (see page 17)
- Gold marker pen

timing Pressing the flowers is what takes the time (about two weeks), but once they have dried you can put together a card in minutes. Choose flowers that aren't too 'fleshy' as they may go mouldy in the press.

message The perfect love greeting – ideal for Valentine's day or for sending a surprise romantic greeting to a loved one.

1 Measure and cut out a rectangle 22 x 26cm (8¾ x 10½in) from white handmade paper, fold in half, then in half again to make a double layer card base.

2 Next, measure and cut out a rectangle 10.5 x 8.5cm (4¼ x 3¼in) from the pink handmade paper. Use a glue stick to attach it in a central position on the card base.

3 Measure and cut out a rectangle 6 x 9cm (2½ x 3½in) from cream textured card. Glue it centrally on the pink handmade paper rectangle.

4 Use the glue stick to attach the pressed rose to the card. Handle the rose carefully as it will be very delicate.

5 Using a ruler, draw a gold border on the white handmade paper around the edge of the card and on the cream card around the rose.

memories of summer

A picnic tea enjoyed on the edge of a field of harvested corn inspired this card. The paper has dried grasses and golden summer flowers layered into it and they create a background for a selection of the grasses and seed heads I picked and pressed that sunny afternoon.

you will need

- Handmade paper impressed with leaves and flowers
- Pencil and metal ruler
- Set square
- Cutting board
- Craft knife
- A5 sheet of tan-coloured handmade paper
- Glue stick
- A5 sheet of cream card
- Selection of dried and pressed seed heads and grasses (see page 17)
- Scissors

timing This card is stylishly simple and easy to make.

message A suitable birthday greeting or thank-you card.

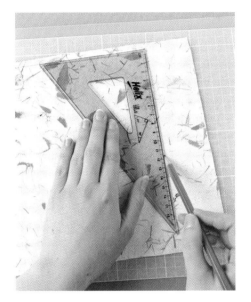

To make the base of the card measure out an area 23 x 20cm (9 x 8in) on the sheet of handmade paper. Place on the cutting board and use the steel ruler and craft knife to cut the shape out. Score and fold the card in half.

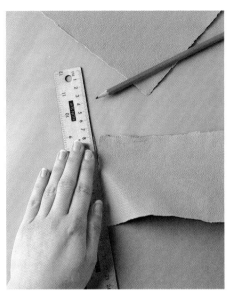

The first layer of the card is made from the tan coloured paper, which forms a frame for the pressed grass picture. Measure a rectangle 10 x 17.5cm (4 x 6¾in) in size and tear the edges along the metal ruler. Apply glue and attach it in a central position on the front of the card base.

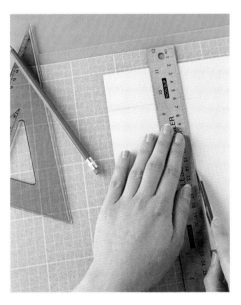

The final layer is cut from the cream card. Measure and cut out a rectangle 9 x 17cm (3½ x 6½in).

Using the glue stick attach the cream rectangle centrally on top of the tan paper.

Sort through your selection of grasses and seed heads and trim them as necessary. Choose some suitable pieces and lay them on the card. When you are happy with the arrangement, glue them to the card.

autumn walk

Take an autumn stroll through the park and make a collection of golden brown, red and green leaves. Once home, press them between the pages of a book for a week or so and when they are dry you will be ready to get to work.

you will need

- A5 sheet of cream card
- Pencil and metal ruler
- A4 sheet of speckled handmade paper
- Cutting board
- Craft knife
- Glue stick
- Selection of pressed leaves (see page 17)
- Black felt tip pen
- Small hole punch
- Thin leather cord

timing This card won't take long to make and you have the added bonus of a walk through crunchy autumn leaves to collect your materials.

message Send a friend a magical autumn greeting.

1 Fold the A5 sheet of cream card in half to make the card base. Use the pencil and ruler to measure an area 14 x 20cm (5½ x 8in) onto the speckled handmade paper. Place the paper onto the cutting board and cut out the measured area using a metal ruler and craft knife.

2 Open out the card base. Apply glue to the speckled paper and attach it in a central position on the card base.

3 Lay a selection of pressed leaves across the card. Take care to choose sympathetic colours and shapes. Do not lay leaves over the central fold as the card will not close properly. When you are happy with the layout, apply glue to the leaves and position them onto the card.

4 Use the black felt tip pen to draw a line of tiny footprints across the front and back of the card.

5 Measure a point halfway down each side of the card. Mark the points with a light pencil mark. Use the hole punch to make two small holes.

6 Thread the leather strip though the two holes and tie a neat bow.

lavender blue

This card could carry a message of love to someone special. It would be particularly meaningful

if the lavender had grown in your own garden. You will need to pick and press the lavender during

the summer months.

you will need

- A4 sheet of lavender blue paper
- Set square
- Pencil
- A5 sheet of white textured card
- Cutting board
- Metal ruler
- Craft knife
- Glue stick
- 3 stems pressed lavender flowers
- Scissors
- PVA glue
- Paint brush
- Pressed heart-shaped seed heads
- Silver paint

timing This card is very quick to assemble. Remember however, that your lavender will take a couple of weeks to press.

message Instead of silver hearts you could use small stars or silver swirls to embellish the card and send it to a friend for a birthday greeting.

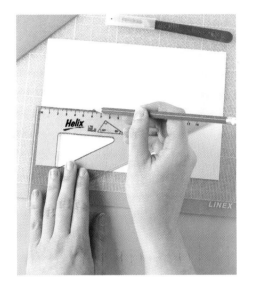

Fold the sheet of lavender blue paper in half to create the card base. Use the set square and pencil to measure a rectangle 6 x 9cm (2½ x 3½in) onto a sheet of white textured card. Place on the cutting board and use your metal ruler and craft knife to cut it out.

Using the glue stick apply glue to the back of the white card rectangle and attach it to the card base in a high central position.

If necessary trim the lavender stems. It is best to keep the stem that will be used in the centre of the card slightly longer than the other two. Coat the back of each stem with PVA glue and position on the card.

I was fortunate to find some heart-shaped seed heads in the garden which I pressed and painted silver. If you can't find anything like this, you might want to cut some small heart shapes from a piece of silver card. Use PVA glue to attach the silver heart shapes to the card.

photo wallet

Make this simple photo wallet greetings card to send to a friend or relative containing a special selection of photographs. It is very simple to make and with the handy ribbon tie has an heirloom feel about it. You might want to decorate the paper wallet using different punched motifs to suit it to your own style.

you will need

- Metal ruler
- Set square
- Pencil
- Large sheet of cream handmade paper
- Cutting board
- Craft knife
- A5 sheet of red paper
- Punch
- Glue stick
- 60cm (24in) red ribbon
- Scissors

timing This gift is very quick to make and will last a lifetime.

message A wonderful gift to send to a friend to remind them of old times.

1 Use the ruler, set square and pencil to mark up a rectangle 25 x 40cm (10 x 15¾in) on the sheet of handmade paper. Cut out the rectangle using the craft knife.

2 Fold the sheet in half lengthways, draw your thumb along the fold to create a sharp edge. Then fold the card in half widthways, press the fold firmly, then open out.

3 Turn the paper over and fold each end into the centre fold. You should now have four equal rectangles; these form the pages of the album.

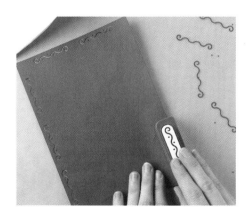

4 Take the sheet of red paper and punch out six decorative edging shapes using your chosen punch. Unfold the card. Use the glue stick to attach a shape to alternate upper corners of each of the four pages closest to you. Then attach a shape to the top left and bottom right corners of the upper left page. This will become the front of the card.

5 Lay the card on the cutting board. Use the craft knife to cut two small slits in two opposing corners of each page. These slits will hold the photographs or pictures in place.

6 Finally fold the album back into shape and use the glue stick to attach the ribbon across the back of the card. Bring the ribbon ends around to the front and tie in a bow.

hanging star

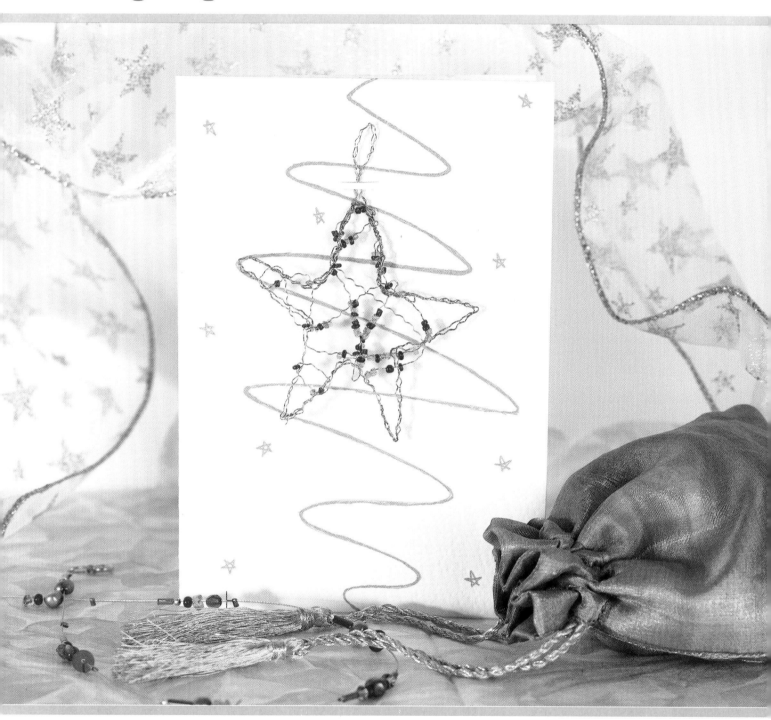

This Christmas card is a jewelled star decoration attached to a white card base decorated with a gold swirl. Even when the star is removed to be hung on the tree, the card is still very pretty.

you will need

- Reel of decorative gold wire
- Scissors
- Metal ruler
- 15 small red beads
- 15 small gold beads
- A5 sheet of white textured card
- Gold pen
- Craft knife
- Cutting board

timing A simple card, but it does take a little time to make as the star decoration is delicate and quite intricate.

message A great card to send to a friend at Christmas time, as they can use the decoration again and again and will always be reminded of the sender.

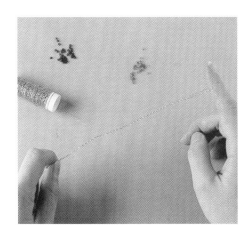

1 Cut a 60cm (24in) length of gold wire. Fold in half and twist the two strands together.

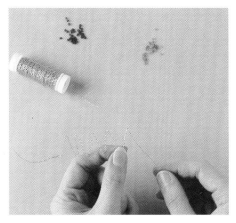

2 Bend the wire into a series of five points, with each side of the point 2cm (¾in) long, leaving a little wire spare at the beginning and end.

3 Form the zigzags into a five-pointed star. Coil the ends of the wire together to hold the star shape in place. Twist the end of the wire around to form a loop. Wrap around to secure and snip off the surplus wire.

4 Thread the beads onto a 20cm (8in) length of wire, alternating red and gold. Hold the bottom of the wire firmly, then attach the top to any point on the star and randomly weave the beaded wire around the star. Twist the end firmly around the star to hold.

5 Fold the sheet of card in half. Using the gold pen, draw a fluid zigzag on the front of the card. Draw small stars on either side.

6 Using the craft knife, make two small parallel slits near the top of the front of the card, 1cm (½in) long. Thread the loop of the star through the slit so it hangs freely.

dreamcatcher

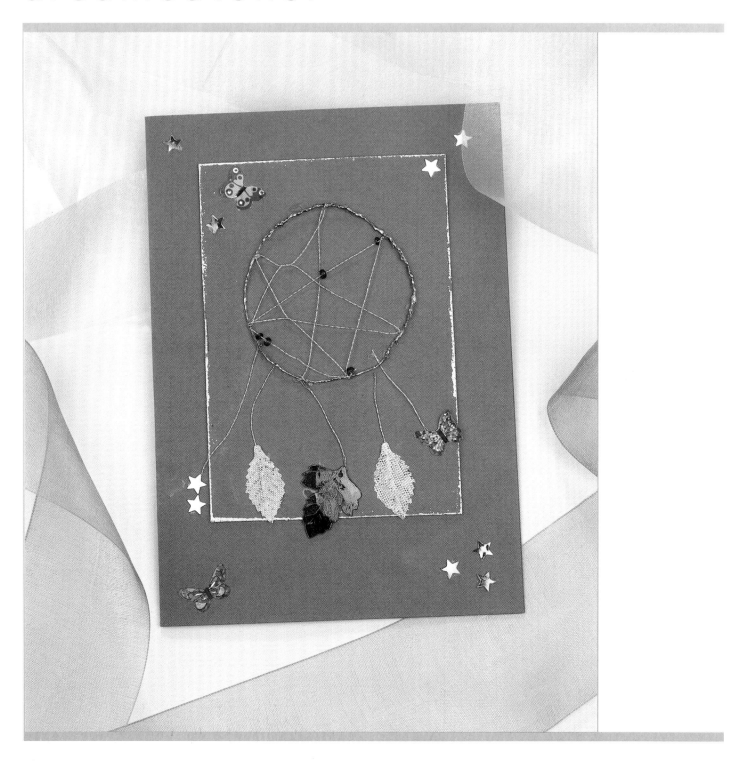

Send this dreamcatcher to a young friend to bring a little magic into his or her life and help slay the dragons that might be troubling their dreams. You could personalize the card by decorating the net with minature items that are significant to the recipient. If you cannot find a suitable bangle, shape a length of thin silver wire into a small circle.

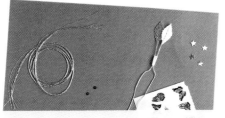

you will need

- 2 A5 sheets of violet card
- Craft knife
- Cutting board
- Metal ruler
- Set square
- Pencil
- Embossing stamp pad
- Silver-white embossing powder
- Precision heat tool
- Glue stick
- Silver thread
- Scissors
- Small silver bangle
- PVA glue
- Paint brush
- 5 small beads
- Selection of foil leaf shapes
- Butterfly stickers
- Silver stars

timing This card takes some time to make, so to ensure a good result, set aside an hour or two when you will not be disturbed.

message A magical card suitable for 'get well' greetings.

1   Score and fold an A5 sheet of violet card to create the card base. Cut a rectangle 7 x 10cm (2¾ x 4in) from the other sheet of violet card. Press the edges of the rectangle into the embossing pad and then dip into the embossing powder. Use the heat tool to set (see page 12).

2   Using the glue stick, cover the back of the decorated card with glue and attach it in an upper central position to the card base. Cut a length of silver thread and tie it to the silver bangle. Use a dab of PVA glue to hold the thread in place.

3   Loop and weave the thread around and across the bangle to create a net effect.

4   Take another short length of thread. Tie a knot in one end, thread on five beads and knot the other end. Tie onto the bangle and weave through the net.

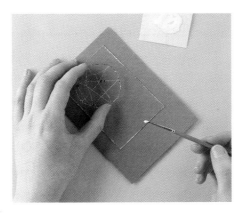

5   When you are happy with the appearance of your dreamcatcher use a little PVA glue to attach it to the card in a high central position.

6   Attach five lengths of thread to the bottom of the dreamcatcher. Place a leaf, star or butterfly at the end of each thread and decorate the corners of the card with butterflies and stars.

tic-tac-toe

A game of three-in-a-row played on this bright yellow gift card decorated with ladybirds and daisies should bring a smile to someone's face. The game board is marked out with green card strips and the ladybirds are stamped onto card, cut out and coloured in with felt tip pen.

you will need

- A4 sheet of yellow card
- A4 sheet of white card
- Pencil and metal ruler
- Cutting board
- Craft knife
- Glue stick
- A5 sheet of green card
- Wavy-edged scissors

- Acetate, 2 x 8cm (¾ x 3¼in)
- Piece of white card, for the counters
- Fine black pen
- Orange and red felt tip pens
- Scissors
- Ladybird stamp
- Black ink pad

timing An hour or two spent making this card will bring fun and laughter into someone's life.

message Send this delightful greeting card to a young friend, and be sure to have a game when next visiting.

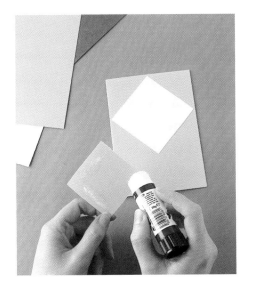

Cut the A4 sheet of yellow card in half. Fold one half in half, this is the card base. Cut out a piece of white card 7 x 7cm (2¾ x 2¾in) and a piece of yellow card 6.5 x 6.5cm (2½ x 2½in). Glue the white square diagonally at the top of the card then stick the yellow square on top.

Cut four narrow strips of green card, each approximately 7cm (2¾in) long. Using the photo for guidance, glue them across the square to create the game board.

Trace and cut out the pocket template on page 141. On the green card draw around the template and cut out the shape. Use wavy-edged scissors to decorate the outer edge.

Glue the pocket surround to the acetate and then glue the pocket to the bottom of the card. The pocket opening should face upwards.

The counters are made from white card. Using the fine black pen, draw seven simple daisy shapes and decorate with orange felt tip pen.

continued ▶

Carefully cut out the daisy shapes, cutting just outside the black line.

Individual flowers and ladybirds make neat gift tags.

Use the ladybird stamp and the black ink pad to print five counters on the remaining piece of white card.

Neatly colour the ladybirds in using the red felt tip pen. Carefully cut them out.

Glue two of the daisies at the top corners of the card and place the rest in the pocket with the ladybirds.

the big day

Romantic pastel colours, golden hearts and a gold embossed stamp neatly enfold a gift of flower petal confetti. This card would make a lovely wedding invitation or wedding gift card.

continued ▶

you will need

- A4 sheet of white textured card
- Pencil and metal ruler
- Craft knife
- Cutting board
- Handmade paper in pastel pink
- Paint brush and water
- Iron and ironing board
- Glue stick
- Stamp with a romantic image
- Embossing stamp pad
- Embossing powder in gold
- Precision heat tool
- Scissors
- Gold foil hearts
- Tweezers
- Gold outliner
- White mulberry paper, 12 x 10cm (4¾ x 4in)
- Hole punch
- Suitable dried flower petals (see page 17)
- Short length of narrow ribbon in palest pink

timing This card takes time and love to make but is well worth it, and once you have made one you might want to set up a production line and make them as wedding invitations.

message Send to newly-weds or as an anniversary card.

1 Cut the A4 sheet of paper in half and fold one half in half; this is the card blank. Using a ruler and the lightest of pencil marks measure a rectangle 13 x 9cm (5 x 3½in) on the handmade paper.

2 Using the paint brush generously dipped in water, paint a water line around the marked rectangle, thoroughly soaking the paper.

3 Carefully tear the rectangle out. Set an iron to medium heat and iron the paper dry. Allow the paper to cool, then use the glue stick to attach it centrally to the card blank.

4 Using your chosen stamp, print the image using an embossing stamp pad onto the white textured card. You may wish to print several images.

Sprinkle the gold embossing powder over the stamped image. Shake off the excess powder onto a piece of scrap paper and then return it to the pot.

Set the embossed image using the heat tool (see page 12). Cut out leaving a narrow border around the image.

Use the glue stick to attach the embossed picture to the card. Once the glue has set, decorate the card with gold foil hearts; pick them up with tweezers, dab them onto the glue stick and place on the card. Frame the embossed image with the gold outliner.

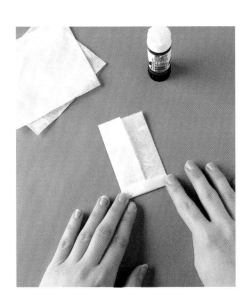

To make the bag of confetti, fold the two sides of the mulberry paper into the centre so they overlap slightly and fold up the base. Glue the edges in place.

Emboss the image on the front of the bag and use a hole punch to make two small holes for the ribbon tie. Fill the bag with flower petals. Thread the ribbon through the holes, tie a bow and use a small dab of glue to attach inside the card.

A matching envelope completes this elegant card.

gallery
general

1 The clean colours of blue and white come together to create this summer greetings card. White gel pen flowers highlight the true blue of this card which is relatively simple to make.

2 A stylish card made from three layers of textured and handmade papers in natural creams and browns, decorated with three perfect feathers and embellished with gold.

3 Simplicity itself, starting with a white textured card blank, a panel of creamy handmade paper edged with gold and decorated with a single pressed flower. The symbols are taken from the 'I Ching' and symbolize creativity.

4 White slightly textured handmade paper provides the backdrop for a powder blue sea, a silver metallic boat and embellishments. A card suitable for most occasions.

5 Tissue paper fish decorated with gel pens on white textured card create this perky little card. Fold the tissue paper in layers before pencilling the fish outline, that way you will end up cutting out a school of fish. Use the same technique when cutting out the rushes.

6 This sunny card will brighten up a birthday morning for someone close to you. The brilliant yellow background and gold and orange borders frame a white daisy painted in fabric paint. Be sure to leave sufficient time for the fabric paint to dry thoroughly before assembling the card.

2

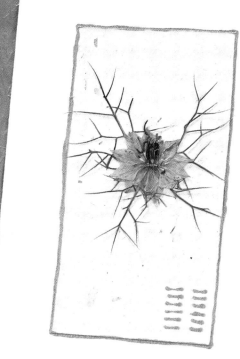

3

5

6

gallery

romance

1 This beautiful pink and white starry translucent paper creates a romantic backdrop for a bunch of pink and silver balloons. Set on white textured paper against a silver panel, the sticker works very well. It is useful to have a selection of stickers available for creating special cards.

2 The perfect card to send congratulations to a newly engaged couple. The background is cut from the palest pink card and a slightly padded silk cushion surrounded by a speckled silver frame holds a faux diamond solitaire ring and a smattering of tiny silver foil hearts.

3 Use red and white card and translucent white striped paper to bring a little stylish romance to someone's life. This Valentine wouldn't look out of place on his or her desk (if left anonymously of course!).

4 This striking card is made from all the bits and pieces that you have in your card-making box. Simple to make yet extremely effective.

5 Layers of white, gold and red papers and a heart-shaped miniature box of chocolates – maybe this card should be attached to a box of the real thing. Use thin card to form the box and modelling clay in shades of brown and cream to make the chocolates.

6 Red heart-shaped blossoms on bright green stalks drawn in green and red gel pens create a sweet little card. The perfect Valentine or congratulations card for newlyweds. Use layers of red and cream card highlighted with red embossing powder.

1

4

2

3

5

6

gallery
christmas

1 Pale mossy green shades of paper, textured white card, silver foil and gel pens have been used to create this sophisticated greetings card. Cut-outs take time and patience to do. Begin by drawing the mistletoe using light pencil strokes as you will need to rub out the pencil marks. Use the gel pens to decorate the card once it has been assembled.

2 A tiny felt Christmas tree embroidered with simple bauble shapes and decorated with a foil star. A special Christmas wish from the scrap box, this card will take a little time to sew.

3 Gold card, red paper and corrugated card were used to create this Christmas greeting. Cutting a window in a card is simple to do and makes it a little more unusual. A truly stylish and simple card to make.

4 Using the same techniques as the Speckled Eggs card on pages 43 to 45, this unusual pink and gold collage of Christmas tree baubles will take time to make. Use gold outliner to decorate the bauble shapes and fine wire to create the loops on each bauble. I think this card is well worth the effort and would be a joy to receive at Christmas time.

5 Party crackers are great at any time of year but especially at Christmas. Cut the cracker from card and decorate with foil and glitter glue. Roll up a piece of tissue paper to make a miniature paper hat and use fabric paint to create the favour. Decorate the card with tiny foil stars and you will have something really special to send out this Christmas.

6 Set on a background of midnight blue card, the snowman stands glittering in the snow. Get the children to help cut out snowmen and make a batch of these cards to send out seasonal greetings.

gallery

children's

1 Bring a smile to someone's face with these bright circus colours: blue corrugated card signifies a clear sky, green, the grassy meadow and the red and yellow stripes remind us of the big top. The jumping jack will dance when the string is pulled.

2 A paper and fabric collage create a springtime rural scene of blue sky, rolling hills and sheep, surrounded by yellow daisies made from fabric paint and green paper.

3 A simple ark cut from papyrus paper and set on green mottled card against a backdrop of golden yellow corrugated card. The delightful animal stickers decorate the scene two by two. Perfect for the nursery and good enough to be kept as a framed memento.

4 Framed by red and yellow layers and decorated with yellow fabric paint and gel pen flower sprigs, is a bright red lollipop tied with a red ribbon bow. Lollipops are not suitable for young children, be sure to check with the child's carer before you deliver the card.

5 I love this fabric collage. The colours are homespun pinks, browns and brick reds. The calico doll has yarn hair attached with glue and her features are drawn on with pencil crayons.

6 A paper rainbow-decorated hot air balloon floats across a summer sky in this paper collage. Tiny gel pen birds soar high above and puffy white paper clouds decorate the scene. The basket is cut from corrugated card.

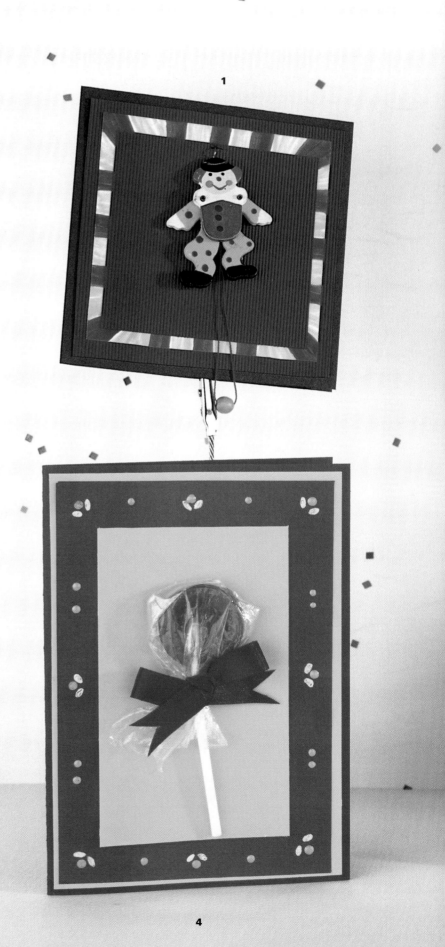

2

3

5

6

templates

The templates shown here are actual size.
They may be easily enlarged or reduced on
a photocopier if you wish to make a larger
or smaller card.

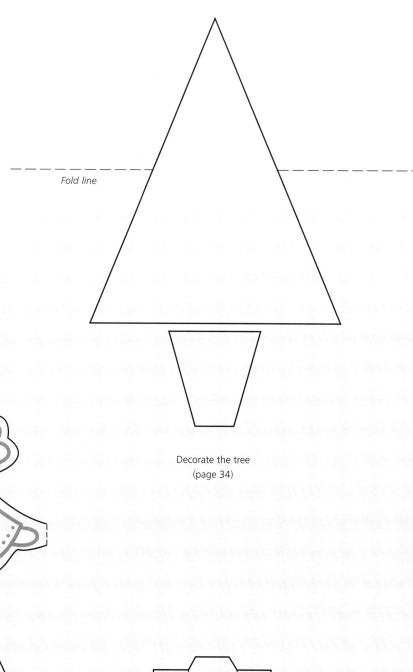

Fold line

Decorate the tree
(page 34)

Host of angels
(page 32)

Gardener's memory album
(page 36)

Spring surprise
(page 40)

Looking through the garden gate
(page 38)

Position tree here

Position tree here

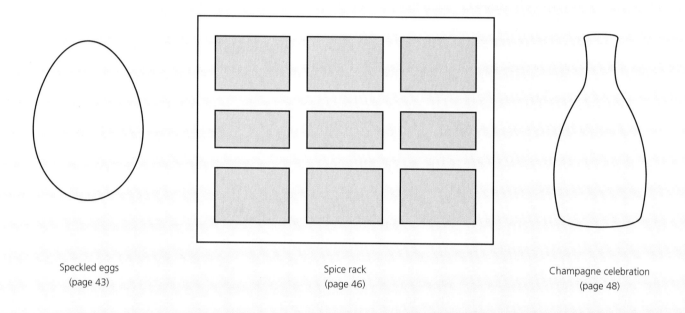

Speckled eggs
(page 43)

Spice rack
(page 46)

Champagne celebration
(page 48)

Pop-up parrots
(page 53)

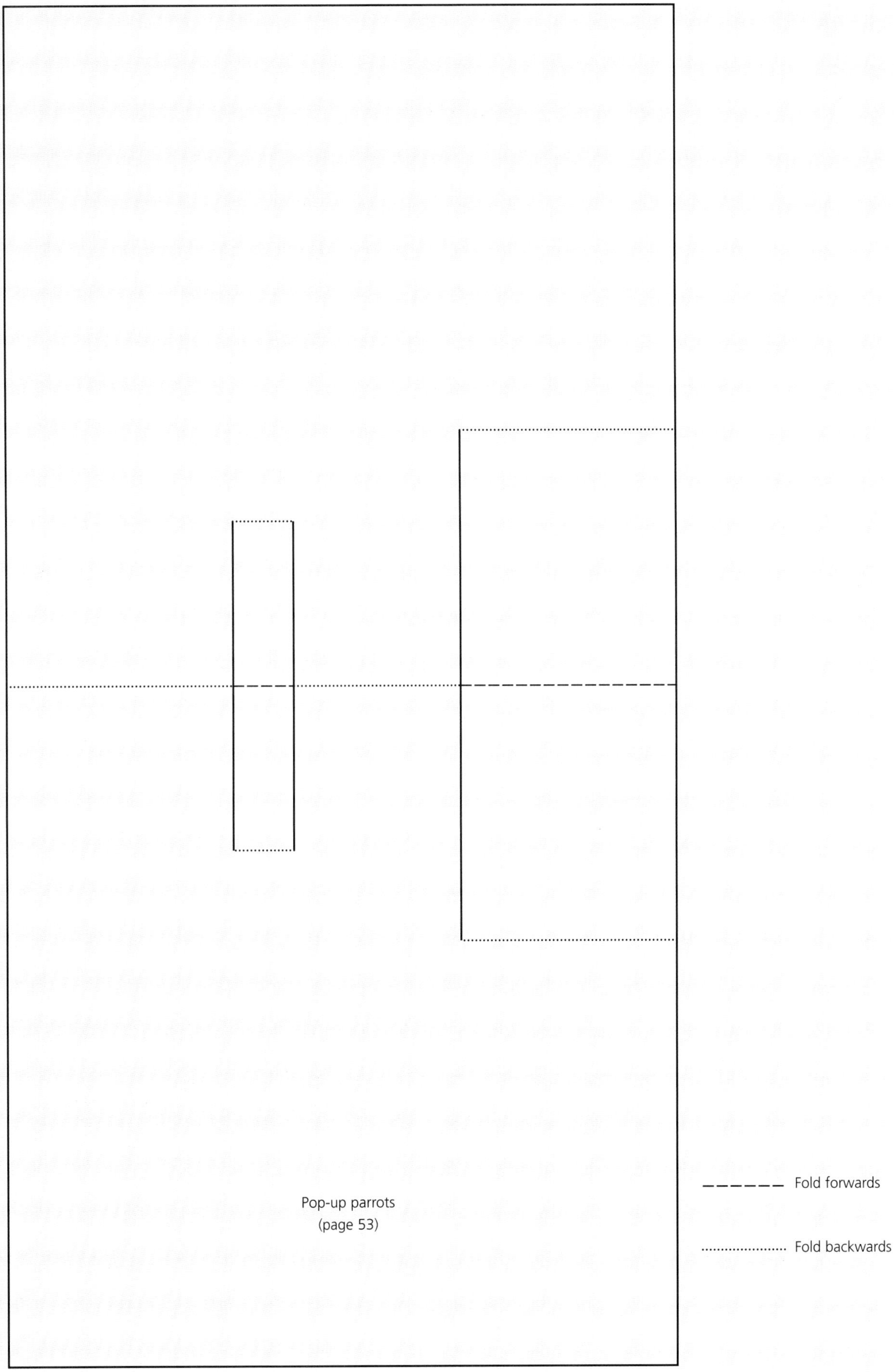

Pop-up parrots
(page 53)

– – – – – – Fold forwards

.... Fold backwards

Oriental flowers
(page 60)

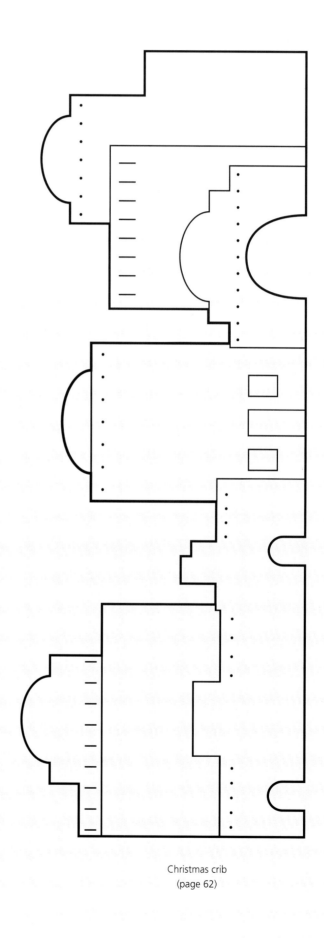

Christmas crib
(page 62)

Glitz and glamour
(page 64)

Lines indicate edge of image

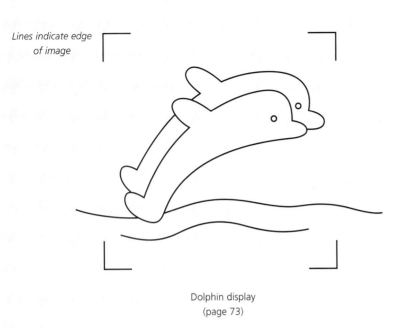

Dolphin display
(page 73)

Poppy field
(page 76)

Robin red breast
(page 66)

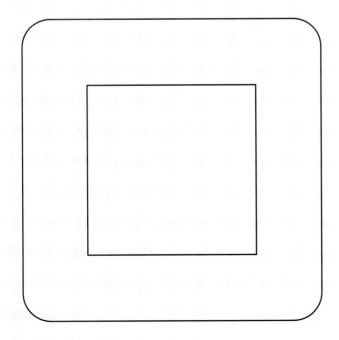

Christmas pudding
(page 82)

Woven ribbon
(page 88)

Scented lavender
(page 84)

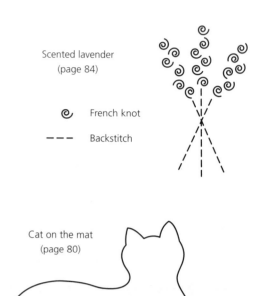

French knot

Backstitch

Cat on the mat
(page 80)

35

30

25

20

15

10

5

0

0   5   10   15   20   25   30   35

Cross-stitch greeting
(page 94)

Dashed lines show
where initials are
positioned; these are
for guidance only,
these outlines should
not be stitched.

Harvest landscape
(page 96)

Underwater scene
(page 98)

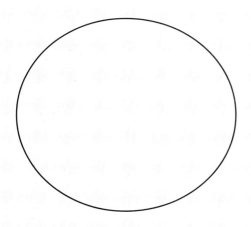

Welcome little stranger
(page 102)

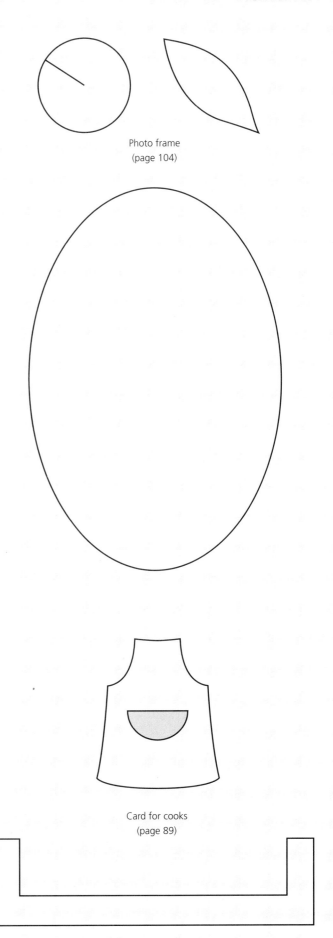

Photo frame
(page 104)

Card for cooks
(page 89)

Tic-tac-toe
(page 120)

suppliers

United Kingdom

Cowling & Wilcox
26-28 Broadwick Street
London W1F 8HX
Tel: 020 7734 5781
Website: www.cowlingandwilcox.com
General craft supplier.

Craft Creations
Ingersoll House
Delamare Road
Cheshunt
Hertfordshire EN8 9ND
Tel: 01992 781 900
Email: enquiries@craftcreations.com
Website: www.craftcreations.com
General craft supplier.

Cranberry Card Company
37 Cromwell Close
Walcote
Lutterworth
Leicestershire LE17 4JJ
Tel: 01455 554 615 / 01443 224 442
Email: info@cranberrycards.co.uk
Website: www.cranberrycards.co.uk
Selection of card, paper and accessories.

Falkiner Fine Papers Ltd
76 Southampton Row
London WC1B 4AR
Tel: 020 7831 1151
*Carries a large range of handmade papers.
Also offers a mail-order service.*

Homecrafts Direct
PO Box 38
Leicester LE1 9BU
Tel: 0845 458 4531
Website: www.homecrafts.co.uk
Email: info@homecrafts.co.uk
*Mail-order service. Selection of handmade
papers and range of craft products.*

L. Cornelissen & Son Ltd
105 Great Russell Street
London WC1B 3RY
Tel: 020 7636 1045

Also:
1A Hercules Street
London N7 6AT
Tel: 020 7281 8870
General craft supplier.

Paperchase
Flagship Store and Main Office
213 Tottenham Court Road
London W1P 9AF
Tel: 020 7467 6200
*Retailers of stationery, wrapping paper and
art materials. Call for your nearest outlet.*

Mail order service
Tel: 0161 839 1500
Website: www.paperchase.co.uk
Email: mailorder@paperchase.co.uk

Plaid UK Ltd
Greenhill Lane
Riddings
Derbyshire DE55 4EX
Tel: 01773 540 808
Email: help@plaiduk.com
Website: www.plaiduk.com
*Mail-order, catalogue; specialists in
stamping materials.*

The English Stamp Company
Worth Matravers
Dorset BH19 3JP
Tel: 01929 439 117
Email: sales@englishstamp.com
Website: www.englishstamp.com
*Suppliers of stamps, paints, inkpads and
handmade paper. Mail order only.*

T N Lawrence
117-119 Clerkenwell Road
London EC1R 5BY
Tel: 020 7242 3534
Website: www.lawrence.co.uk
*Carries a large range of papers as well as
general artist's materials.*

The Stencil Store
20/21 Heronsgate Road
Chorleywood

Herts WD3 5BN
Tel: 01923 285577
Email: mail@stencilstore.com
Website: www.stencilstore.com
*Supply wide range of stencil designs.
Phone for nearest store or to order
catalogue.*

Australia

Artwise Amazing Paper
186 Enmore Road
Enmore, NSW 2042
Tel: 02 9519 8237

Eliza Stamping
18 Segarta Circuit
Ferntree Gully, VIC 3156
Tel: 03 9752 4201
Website:
www.elizastamping.alphalink.com.au

Lincraft
Website: www.lincraft.com.au
*General craft supplier. Stores throughout
Australia*

Myer Centre, Rundle Mall
Adelaide, SA 5000
Tel: 02 8231 6611

Myer Centre, Queen Street
Brisbane, QLD 4000
Tel: 07 3221 0064

Canberra Centre, Bunda Street
Canberra, ACT 2601
Tel: 02 6257 4516

107 Liverpool Street
Hobart, TAS 7000
Tel: 03 6234 4241

Australia on Collins
Melbourne, VIC 3000
Tel: 03 9650 1609

Imperial Arcade, Pitt Street
Sydney, NSW 2000
Tel: 02 9221 5111

Paper Fantasy
256a Charters Towers Road
Hermit Park, QLD 4812
Tel: 07 4725 1272

Paperwright
124 Lygon Street
Carlton, VIC 3053
Tel: 03 9663 8747

Spotlight
Tel: 1800 656 256
Website: www.spotlight.com.au
General craft supplier. Call for nearest store.

South Africa

Arts, Crafts and Hobbies
72 Hibernia Street
George 6529
Tel / Fax: 044 874 1337
Mail-order service available.

Art Mates
Shop 313, Musgrave Centre
124 Musgrave Road
Durban 4000
Tel / Fax: 021 201 0094

Bowker Arts and Crafts
52 4th Avenue
Newton Park
Port Elizabeth 6001
Tel: 041 365 2487
Fax: 041 365 5306

Crafty Supplies
Shop UG 104, The Atrium
Main Road, Claremont 7700
Tel: 021 671 0286
Fax: 021 671 0308

Creative Papercraft
64 Judd Street
Horizon
Roodepoort 1724
Tel / Fax: 763 5682

E. Sweikerdt (Pty) Ltd
590 Souter Street
Pretoria West
Tel: 012 884 8282
Fax: 012 327 0710
Mail-order service available.

**L&P Stationery and Artists'
Requirements**
College Square, Shop 10
Bloemfontein 9301
Tel: 051 430 8608
Fax: 051 430 4102

Le Papier du Port
Gardens Centre
Cape Town 8000
Tel: 021 462 4796
Fax: 021 461 9281
Mail-order service available.

Scarab Paper
P.O Box 123
Sedgefield 6573
Tel 044 343 2455
Fax: 044 343 1828
Website: www.home.mweb.co.za
E-mail: scarabpaper@mweb.co.za

New Zealand

Brush & Palette
50 Lichfield Street
Christchurch
Tel / Fax: 03 366 3088

Fine Art Papers
200 Madras Street
Christchurch
Tel: 03 379 4410
Fax: 03 379 4443

Gordon Harris Art Supplies
4 Gillies Ave
Newmarket
Auckland
Tel: 09 520 4466
Fax: 09 520 0880

Littlejohns
170 Victoria Street
Wellington
Tel: 04 385 2099
Fax: 04 385 2090

Studio Art Supplies
81 Parnell Rise
Parnell
Auckland
Tel: 09 377 0302
Fax: 09 377 7657

Websters
44 Manners Street
Wellington
Tel: 04 384 2134
Fax: 04 384 2968

index